Céline's Imaginative Space

American University Studies

Series II
Romance Languages and Literature

Vol. 42

PETER LANG
New York · Bern · Frankfurt am Main · Paris

Jane Carson

Céline's Imaginative Space

PETER LANG
New York · Bern · Frankfurt am Main · Paris

Library of Congress Cataloging-in-Publication Data

Carson, Jane
   Céline's imaginative space

   (American university studies. Series II, Romance
languages and literature ; vol. 42)
   Bibliography: p.
   Includes index.
      1. Céline, Louis-Ferdinand, 1894–1961—Criticism
and interpretation.   2. Space and time in literature.
3. Picaresque literature, French—History and
criticism. I. Title. II. Series.
   PQ2607.E834Z615   1987
         843'.912   86-27668
   ISBN 0-8204-0308-3
   ISSN 0740-9257

CIP-Kurztitelaufnahme der Deutschen Bibliothek

Carson, Jane:
Céline's imaginative space / Jane Carson. – New
York; Bern; Frankfurt am Main; Paris: Lang,
1987.
   (American University Studies: Ser. 2,
   Romance Languages and Literature; Vol. 42)
   ISBN 0-8204-0308-3

NE: American University Studies / 02

323374

Printed by Weihert-Druck GmbH, Darmstadt, West Germany

ACKNOWLEDGMENTS

Parts of this book have previously appeared in print; they are reprinted by permission. This material was first published in the following articles:

"Céline: The Fire in the Night." *Symposium*, Vol. 35, No. 2 (Summer 1981), 117–130. Reprinted with permission of the Helen Dwight Reid Educational Foundation. Published by Heldref Publications, 4000 Albemarle St., N.W., Washington, D.C. 20016. Copyright © 1981.

"The Biomorphic Structure of Céline's Imaginative Space." *Degré Second*, No. 8 (July 1984), 13–17. Copyright © Degré Second 1984.

TABLE OF CONTENTS

INTRODUCTION

The picaresque novel is a peculiar elaboration of the quest theme as we know it in Western literature, and since its first appearance in Spain this episodic pseudo-autobiographical form, featuring a protagonist who has nothing about him of the hero, has inspired innumerable imitations and variations. Unlike the hero of myth, the pícaro is no better endowed than other people, he does not cross the threshold into the other world, and the only boon he gains to pass on to his fellows is the tale of his own adventures, edifying though it may be. In this respect his "quest" is an archetypal failure. Although he lacks a sense of sacred mission, the pícaro, driven by a desire to rise in society, still seems to be engaged in a search. Inasmuch as he usually rejects, in the end, the goal of wealth he has been pursuing, the only result of his journey is a need to communicate his peripatetic history to a reader. The pícaro's history is varied, scatological, darkly humorous, morally ambiguous. He narrates it himself. The outcome of his quest is the writing of his novel.

The narrators of all of Céline's novels, from the Bardamu of *Voyage au bout de la nuit* to the doctor of *Rigodon*, share a desire to recount a journey which, as they are the first to point out, leads to no magic solution, no shining Grail.

> Notre vie est un voyage
> Dans l'hiver et dans la Nuit,
> Nous cherchons notre passage
> Dans le ciel où rien ne luit.
>
> (Our life is a journey
> Through winter and Night,
> We search for our way
> In a sky without light.)
>
> epigraph, *Voyage au bout de la nuit*

Despite the lack of light, they observe very closely the evils surrounding them, and they often participate in a way suggesting the ambivalent moral stance which has been seen as fundamental to the picaresque.[1]

Although A. A. Parker's definition of the picaresque genre totally excludes such works as *Voyage au bout de la nuit*, his discussion of Alemán's *Guzmán de Alfarache* exactly summarizes Céline's thesis. He points out that the novel presents a comprehensive panorama of society, with the emphasis on the corruption of all men. Their selfishness is not due to specific historical conditions, nor is it limited to Alemán's time and country. "Institutions change, men remain the same."[2] The delinquent protagonist, no exception to the

general run of humanity, is the representative of mankind.
Parker insists on the following four points as essential to
the true picaresque: the pícaro is of disreputable origin,
he has a profound desire to rise and become a gentleman, instead he becomes a social delinquent, and after sinking to
the depths of depravity he experiences a religious conver-
sion.

It is important to keep in mind that Parker's discussion
of the picaresque is confined to very narrow limits--150
years of European literary examples. He considers this the
only period which is truly picaresque. I prefer to use this
limited definition because the word picaresque has become so
vague that in our times almost any novel in which a journey
is undertaken may be called picaresque.

Céline's work is almost a parody of the four points
listed above: his protagonist is of respectable middle-class
parentage, his greatest desire is to descend to the depths of
human experience, he becomes not an outlaw but a moral delinquent, and he denies the possibility of a final spiritual exaltation. Step by step, Céline's narrators follow this distorted version of the picaresque, with the result that his
assembled novels may be taken as the history of the inverted
picaresque adventure of the future novelist. The frustrated
quest forms the basis for the journey in each of Céline's
novels, some of which adhere to the picaresque pattern more
closely than others. The point that each novel seems to
make, and for which the series of novels stands as evidence,

is that the protagonist gains nothing from life but a story to tell.

In the thirty years (1932-61) during which the narrator gradually becomes the doctor/novelist identified as the writer, the quest theme in its picaresque variant remains predominant. My purpose in the following pages is to describe the imaginative space in which this picaresque adventure unfolds. My study is based on certain primary clusters of images related to space, movement, and the concept of time. The first and third chapters discuss the structure of conscious and subconscious space, the former an exitless labyrinth, the latter an underground which serves as womb for the genesis of the work of art. The underground is reached, as the second chapter shows, by falling. The fall and subsequent exploration of the underground is the inspiration for the writing of the novel. In the fourth chapter, an analysis of the images related to fire shows that the narrator sees himself as a fire-maker and the work of art as a flame. This light fitfully illuminates a world of otherwise unrelieved blackness. The fifth chapter deals with the perception of time as endless waiting and the end of the journey, death.

Although a generation of young people which has grown up reading Queneau, Beckett, and the nouveaux romanciers finds Voyage au bout de la nuit tame and almost without linguistic originality, in 1932 the novel was considered highly innovative, and its use of spoken syntax, street slang, and popular obscenities marked a decided break with the rigid traditions

of written French. However, Céline's reputation was serious-
ly damaged by the anti-Semitic pamphlets he published during
World War II, and critical articles after the war devoted
much space to proving once and for all that he did or did not
collaborate with the Germans. He also suffered from his
readers' persistent and willful confusion of his life and
fiction--complicated by his habit of making contradictory and
distorted statements about his past--with the result that his
novels have been classified with "those works whose authors,
although they are writing undisguised autobiographies, call
them 'novels'".[3] Thus critics have been forced to write articles dispelling the misconceptions, arising from his fictional "autobiography," that Céline was trepanned during the
war, that he grew up in grinding poverty, and that his mother
was a cripple.

The first book-length critical studies appeared soon after his death in 1961, and the recent proliferation of articles, dissertations, and biographies attest to his renewed
popularity. The critics tend to adopt a stance either sympa-
thetic to the point of eulogy or highly censorious. The two
extremes are reflected in such titles as Céline and His Vision[4] and Céline, Man of Hate.[5]

In his discussion of spatial imagery,[6] Gilbert Schilling
emphasizes the hostility of the space in which the hero is
engaged in a quest for refuge; he eventually retreats into
the "imaginaire." In the following pages I will show that
the protagonist does not retreat, after unhappy experiences

in the real world, to the world of the imagination: he is already ensconced in the imagination from the start, and he never leaves it. He perceives conscious space as a labyrinth without an exit, a paranoid space in which he is constantly surrounded by walls. This is very different from Plutarch's labyrinth myth, where Theseus stalks the Minotaur, kills it with his bare hands, escapes with the woman who helped him, and is acclaimed a hero. Céline makes it very clear from the outset that there are no heroes. The only people who take death lightly are those who don't know what it means. Céline's narrators feel lost and hunted. Women refuse to help them--in fact, women betray them--and they meet not one, but many monsters.

From conscious space we move below the surface to subconscious space. The transition is abrupt, and it is a descent, therefore the second chapter is a discussion of falls. We are concerned with a fall from a waking to a dream world, and the obvious parallel is Alice in Wonderland. Very often after falling Céline's narrators get up and tell someone their story. The fall gives them the impetus to begin narrating. In Normance the narrator falls down the elevator shaft at the very beginning of the novel. Carried bleeding up to his apartment, he tells his story--the novel--which is clearly the raving of a man who fell on his head. Céline's characters also often murder other characters by pushing them down the stairs, or under trains, or into cesspools. The push is a relatively small gesture to obtain such far-reach-

ing results. The murderer, never apprehended or even pursued, disposes of another character and changes the course of
the action much as a writer, by pushing his pen, creates a
world in which he can annihilate a character simply by drawing a line through his name.

The subterranean world is the underground we know from
so many myths. It has a certain womb-like atmosphere and
seems to offer shelter, but this is an illusion. It is above
all an intestinal image. The metro, for example, which is
the Underground in London, is decidedly a metaphor for the
intestines. The work of the intestines is the last stage in
the digestive process, similar to the creative process, in
which the writer digests experience and produces the written
work. Certainly something is born in the underground: this
is the novel.

The novel in fact sheds light in the darkness of Céline's world. In the fourth chapter I explore the metaphorical consequences of equating fire with the written word. I
set out to determine the function of writing as it appears in
the images related to fire-makers. I find that Céline's
fires either consume garbage, or flow like lava, or draw insects like a candle flame. This suggests some comparisons
between writing and suicide. The destructive impulse of the
writer, which may be turned against himself either when he
throws himself from a great height or when he throws himself
into a flame, may also be turned against others when he
throws bombs or sets fires. In Normance Céline comes very

close to portraying the writer as a prophet who writes with letters of fire in the sky. Although it is a painter who paints the sky with fire, the transcription of the scene is a linguistic tour de force conveying the god-like powers of the writer.

The imaginative journey takes us from the labyrinth to the underground--by falling--and there we find fire. The last chapter concerns the end of the journey, death. "Waiting for Dawn" is waiting for death, because dawn is the time of executions. The many sleepless nights the narrators spend waiting for dawn illustrate the fact that time is conceived as waiting: waiting for an end, waiting for death. For Céline, there is nothing after death, and life is merely filling the time while waiting. There are ways of passing the time which are more acceptable than others: travel is a good example. Writing is also sanctioned as a form of mental travel. As long as time is perceived only as waiting for an end, no end can ever come, because if it does, one is no longer waiting and can no longer perceive time passing. The perception of time in Céline excludes the concept of ends. After death there is no perception of time. Before death there are no ends.

Céline's novels fall into groups of two or three either by subject matter or because they were published as two volumes with the same title. To avoid confusion I refer to them by the following titles: <u>Voyage</u> <u>au</u> <u>bout</u> <u>de</u> <u>la</u> <u>nuit</u> and <u>Mort</u> <u>à</u> <u>crédit</u>, <u>Guignol's</u> <u>Band</u> and <u>Le</u> <u>Pont</u> <u>de</u> <u>Londres</u>, <u>Féerie</u> <u>pour</u>

une _autre_ _fois_ and _Normance_, _D'un_ _Château_ _l'autre_, _Nord_, and _Rigodon_. The four novels (_Voyage_ _au_ _bout_ _de_ _la_ _nuit_, _Guignol's_ _Band_, _Normance_, and _Nord_) from which my examples are drawn include one from each of the first three thematic pairs and one from the final trilogy.7 The quality of the writing is uneven; if _Normance_ is generally conceded to be one of his weakest, _Voyage_ _au_ _bout_ _de_ _la_ _nuit_ (hereafter _Voyage_ or _V_), first published in 1932, is considered by many to be Céline's best work, if not his only work of any value. It is certainly the most widely read and, despite its stylistic innovations, the most traditional.

The protagonist is Bardamu, a young medical student who joins the army to see what war is like; he discovers that it is horrible and incomprehensible. On a dangerous nocturnal reconnaissance mission he meets Robinson, a fellow Frenchman who, like Bardamu, believes in saving his own skin. Bardamu is wounded and returns to Paris to recover. There he has an affair with the American nurse Lola, and later Musyne, a lightsome violinist. Discharged from the military, he leaves for Africa on the ship _Amiral_ _Braqueton_. In the French colony Bambola-Bragamance, he is hired to replace a trader in an isolated jungle post. His predecessor, who turns out to be Robinson, makes off with the cash in the middle of the night. Bardamu falls ill, burns his hut, and travels to a nearby Spanish colony, where a helpful priest sells him as a slave to the captain of a galley leaving for America. In New York Bardamu escapes and runs off to explore the city, where he lives in the enormous hotel Laugh Calvin and looks up Lola to ask for money. Later he works on an assembly line for Ford Motor Company in Detroit, until he is rescued by Molly, a kind-hearted prostitute who offers to support him. However, after meeting Robinson again, Bardamu decides to return to France.

In Part Two Bardamu has completed his medical studies and set up practice in Rancy, a poor suburb of Paris. He does not attract many patients, and he has serious financial difficulties. A couple named Henrouille offers him a thousand francs to certify that the husband's mother is mentally ill. He refuses, but his friend Robinson agrees to set up a bomb to make her death look accidental. Instead, the bomb goes off in his face and Robinson is blinded. He and the old lady are sent to Toulouse to make their living showing tourists through a vault full of mummified bodies. Bardamu leaves Rancy and works briefly as an extra during the intermission entertainment in a movie theater. He goes to Toulouse to visit Robinson, but leaves hurriedly when he learns that Robinson has pushed old lady Henrouille down the steps to the vault, killing her. Bardamu is hired to work in an insane asylum in a Paris suburb, and when the director becomes rather crazy himself and sets off on a long journey, Bardamu takes over the establishment. One day Robinson reappears. He has regained his sight and left his fiancée Madelon, who nevertheless follows him to Paris. In an attempt to restore harmony, Bardamu takes his nurse Sophie, Madelon, and

Robinson to an amusement park one Sunday. Exasperated by Robinson's indifference, Madelon shoots him and flees into the night.

Guignol's Band (G-B), 1944, is the companion to Le Pont de Londres (or Guignol's Band II). The protagonist, Ferdinand, is jobless in London during the First World War. He barhops with Borokrom, a piano player, evades Inspector Matthew of Scotland Yard, and visits Cascade, a souteneur inundated with women whose pimps are leaving to enlist in the French army. A fight breaks out between two of the women; one of them is hospitalized for a knife-wound. After Ferdinand has spent the money he borrowed from Cascade, he looks for Borokrom at the house of Titus van Claben, a pawnbroker. At the end of a wild evening during which they smoke drugs, Boro and Ferdinand force Claben to swallow his gold and throw him down the stairs. Leaving the body in the cellar with Ferdinand and Delphine (Claben's maid), Boro closes the trapdoor, then throws a bomb which sets fire to the house. Ferdinand and Delphine escape, but Boro tells Cascade that it was Ferdinand who killed Claben. One day Ferdinand meets Mille-Pattes, who urges him to return and tell Cascade the true story; instead, Ferdinand pushes Mille-Pattes from the subway platform under the oncoming train. Then he goes to the French embassy and tries to enlist, but they refuse him because he has already been discharged with an 80% disability pension. Finally, he meets Sosthène, a former touring magician, who engages him to leave for Tibet to search for the

"Tara-Tohé, Flower of Dream" which imparts mystical powers to its possessor, as soon as money can be found to finance the expedition.

While _Normance_ (_N_), 1952, also called _Féerie_ _pour_ _une_ _autre_ _fois_ _II_, is probably the least successful of Céline's novels (apart from _Casse-pipe_, unpublished during his life-time), the most repetitive and static, and in any case the least rewarding to wade through, it is one of the most complex from the standpoint of imagery. The handful of charac-ters are practically indistinguishable one from another, the action can be reduced to an almost uninterrupted climbing up and down of stairs with much screaming of insults, the style is so repetitive that whole pages appear to be more or less interchangeable. For these very reasons it is possible to see the novel as an extended metaphor with Jules playing the role of the artist, the limited scope of the action as a con-cise picture of the workings of the creative mind, the char-acters as embodying the writer's fears. Not a single inci-dent is realistic, nor does the novel hold the slightest in-terest as fantasy; only as an artistic game, a display of the writer's virtuosity, can the reader assimilate these pages, and his attention is more likely to be held by the colorful, evocative language than anything else.

The doctor-narrator first announces that he has just fallen down the elevator shaft in a Paris apartment building. His wife and friends carry him back up the stairs to their apartment just as an air attack begins. They make their way down the shaking stairs again, dodging falling furniture, to find their neighbors collected on the first floor hiding under a table. Jules, the paraplegic painter who had supposedly seduced the doctor's wife in the first volume, _Féerie pour une autre fois_, is on top of a "moulin" (variously interpreted as the Moulin de la Galette or an anachronistic windmill), apparently directing the bombardment. In order to revive Delphine, Normance's wife, the tenants use Normance as a battering ram to smash the door of an apartment where they expect to find a bottle of vulnerary. Later they toss his body down the elevator shaft. The doctor returns to his apartment. His friend Ottavio, in search of water, breaks a hole in the wall through which they crawl into the building next door. There, in a room undamaged by bombing, with a dead body in the kitchen and another in the bathroom, they discover the actor Norbert, waiting, he says, for the Pope and other dignitaries to arrive for dinner. Ottavio carries the doctor down the stairs just as the siren sounds for another air attack.

Nord, 1960, is more tightly constructed than any of the other three novels. The narration is straightforward, chronological, less episodic than _Voyage_, less discursive than most of Céline's works. With World War II as the background, the questing activities of the characters have an immediate object: asylum. This confers on the novel a continuity lacking in _Guignol's Band_ and motivates a flight in other ways resembling Bardamu's. This is the second volume of Céline's final trilogy, presenting a highly implausible version of his escape from occupied France through Germany toward Denmark. The story begins in Baden-Baden, where a number of wealthy refugees are collected at the Brenner Hotel. The doctor is warned by the German authorities to take the train to Berlin, where he, his wife, and their friend Le Vigan have so many difficulties obtaining visas that they seek out Harras, a high-ranking medical official who takes them first to the sumptuous subterranean Reichsgesundt, then to Zornhof, a little village on the steppe, far from Berlin, supposedly safer. The doctor spends his days looking for food and avoiding the traps set for him by the eccentric and unaccountably hostile inhabitants. One day the elderly Count von Leiden, the owner of the manor, rides off on his horse to join the war. Some time later he is found at the bottom of a hole, severely beaten. While the entire neighborhood is attending a gypsy performance, the count dies, and both the local Landrat and the count's son, a paraplegic, are discovered drowned in cesspools. Harras reappears and the whole crazy lot are packed off to a distant castle. Dr. Céline and his party move on.

It goes without saying that the above plot summaries are mere skeletal reflections of the original works and are not intended to serve as more than a preliminary guide for the journey to come. The spaces of the imagination are vast and not easily charted. What follows is essentially a history of my own exploration of Céline's imaginative space. Like Thu-

cydides, I have described nothing but what I have seen with
my own eyes.

Notes

[1]Christine J. Whitbourn ("Moral Ambiguity in the Spanish Picaresque Tradition," in _Knaves and Swindlers_, ed. C. J. Whitbourn, London: Hull Univ., 1974) maintains that novels in which there is a strong consciousness of right and wrong fall outside the picaresque tradition.

[2]_Literature and the Delinquent: The Picaresque Novel in Spain and Europe, 1599-1758_ (Edinburgh: Edinburgh Univ. Press, 1967), p. 38.

[3]Sharon Spencer, _Space, Time and Structure in the Modern Novel_ (Chicago: Swallow Press, 1971), p. 53.

[4]Erika Ostrovsky, _Céline and His Vision_ (New York: NYU Press, 1967).

[5]Bettina L. Knapp, _Céline, Man of Hate_ (University, AL: Univ. of Alabama Press, 1974).

[6]"Espace et angoisse dans _Voyage au bout de la nuit_," _Revue des Lettres Modernes_, No. 398-402 (1974), 57-80.

[7]Page numbers throughout this study are from the following editions: _Voyage au bout de la nuit_, Bibliothèque de la Pléiade (Paris: Gallimard, 1962); _Guignol's Band_, Gallimard, 1952; _Normance_, Gallimard, 1954; _Nord_, Bibliothèque de la Pléiade (Paris: Gallimard, 1960) rev. text 1974. All translations, unless otherwise noted, are my own.

I

THE LABYRINTH

Surrounded by city streets, hospital and hotel corridors, jungle paths, and metro tunnels, in every part of the world Bardamu and his successors, Ferdinand and the doctor, feel lost in a maze of narrow pathways, hemmed in by walls. The halls of the Hotel Laugh Calvin in New York, the wards of the "London Freeborn Hospital," the waterways in Africa, are all examples of the labyrinthine structure of space as they experience it. The labyrinth is not only Céline's metaphor for external space; it is also an image for one's perception of the body--from brains to bowels, from the circulatory system to the web of nerves, the body may be pictured as a collection of narrow, winding, tunnel-like passages suggesting to the imagination an extensive internal network of twisting and branching paths. Céline's characters are thus trapped in an analog of the physical body.

Their space is unquestionably enclosed; everywhere they turn they come up against walls. The dominant image of

Voyage has been described as the "rat in a trap."[1] But although their space is confining, all of Céline's narrators
are in constant motion, from continent to continent in Voyage, from castle to castle in later works. The tunnel (such
as we see in Rigodon) is the model for enclosed space allow-
ing movement; the branching tunnel adds the necessity for
choice in movement, increasing the nightmare feeling by forc-
ing the individual to feel responsible for the path he
chooses. As Bachelard says, "Il hésite au milieu d'un chemin
unique"[2] ("He hesitates faced with a single path").

The fact that space is perceived as labyrinthine does
not necessarily mean that it is physically confining: "If
the labyrinth is the archetypal order of things outside the
temple, if it is the basic image of profane space, then its
form is to be defined not so much as a material setting
(trees, rocks, streams, etc.) as a general condition of unmapped disorder."[3] The labyrinth in Spenser, says Angus
Fletcher, is a dense forest; in Eliot it is a wasteland. It
is sufficient that space be characterized by the absence of
"ordre et beauté" for it to be perceived as chaotic and
threatening. Is it possible that, haunted by devious thought
patterns and universal feelings of persecution, people are
creating space (cities, hospitals, and highways) resembling
their inner nightmare? The fear of maze-like disorder in
other than man-made space (forests, deserts, and mountains)
implies that this inner network is being projected on the
world, that people filter their perception of their surround-

ings through this labyrinth image.   Seeing "unmapped disorder" as a labyrinth is to give it structure; writing about a
labyrinth is a further structuring of chaotic experience.
The written work, at least in its traditional form, is by its
very nature an ordered presentation of material.   The subject
may be disorder, but the fact that the work fills a specified
number of pages which may be read and reread at will provides
reassuring evidence that experience can be organized.

The traditional characters of the Western myth of the
labyrinth are Theseus, the Minotaur, and Ariadne.   The role
of guide, properly belonging to the thread which led Theseus
out of the maze, has generally been attributed to Ariadne;
she has assumed the position of savior of mankind.   She is,
if not Woman, then at least the anima, with all the ensuing
androgynous combinations that should lead to a state of primal wholeness.   Where Art is the rescuing thread, the Muse is
female; her redemptive powers attest to the continuing preva-
lence of the Earth Mother image.   The redemptive role of art
will be discussed in a later chapter.   The basic configura-
tion I shall examine in this chapter is a triad: potential
victim, monster, and savior-elect: woman.

Plutarch, in his life of Theseus, disposes of the entire
labyrinth episode in a single sentence.   "When he arrived at
Crete, as most of the ancient historians as well as poets
tell us, having a clue of thread given him by Ariadne, who
had fallen in love with him, and being instructed by her how
to use it so as to conduct him through the windings of the

labyrinth, he escaped out of it and slew the Minotaur, and sailed back, taking along with him Ariadne and the young Athenian captives."[4] Nevertheless, the brief incident has so captured the imagination of writers over the years that in the twentieth century a new surge of fiction has incorporated the labyrinth as a major image, even in the titles: <u>Dans le labyrinthe</u>, <u>Thésée</u>, <u>Le Minotaure</u>.[5] The labyrinth is the perfect setting for a character with a persecution complex, like Kafka's protagonists, or Céline's. Céline's scapegoat mentality has become a cliché, but his original thesis is not that one man has been singled out to purge humanity of its sins, but rather that all men are hunted, all playing tag with the Minotaur, with their lives at stake. P. S. Day evokes the myth of the labyrinth in his discussion of <u>Normance</u>, affirming that Céline (the doctor) is Theseus, Arlette (Lili) Ariadne.[6] I wish to discuss the labyrinth as a conception of space in which Theseus flees and Ariadne dances. Man is the hunted, and each man believes his situation to be unique. In his solitude he looks to Woman, so different from himself, for help, but he receives none. He assumes that she is withholding information out of malice.

From the quarry's point of view, everything which is not himself may be the hunter. His life is governed by fear; his defense will be flight or freezing to escape notice. As J.-P. Richard points out, the persecuted one imagines himself to be always visible; this leads Richard to postulate an open space as the scene of Céline's journey.[7] However, this hypothesis is incompatible with the ambushes and chases connected with the hunt, for which the forest, a natural labyrinth, is a much more suitable setting. In any case, this is not the labyrinth where Theseus boldly stalks the Minotaur and kills him by smiting him with his fists. In this labyrinth Theseus is only trying to save his own skin. He will avoid confrontation with the monster as long as possible, and in his panic he will see danger everywhere. He will flee, he will freeze, but his progress toward death will be inexorable.

The predator manifests himself in many ways. Death is the most obvious enemy, but it is not the only one. The self, since its choices limit one's scope of activity and possibilities for escape, is an enemy. The city is a dangerous, malodorous animal whose streets form an internal labyrinth. The labyrinth itself is an enemy, as surely as if it held no Minotaur.

The third character, Ariadne, or woman, guided Theseus out of the labyrinth only to be abandoned by him. Céline's women generally offer very dangerous advice which the narrator never follows. He admires their physical beauty and grace of movement, but comes to the conclusion that whatever secret they may have for salvation is restricted to the sisterhood.

Thésée traqué

The picaresque hero of Céline's novels is a traveler. He is always a foreigner, "un étranger," always has difficulty understanding the behavior of those about him, as if he belonged to another race. This is a familiar technique of satire, in which an outsider observes society and reports on it from his own point of view. Ignorant at first, he gradually develops, through experience and deliberate exploration, a tentative model to explain the structure of the space he lives in.

For Bardamu, it is his war experience which first teaches him the ways of the world. He quickly learns never to expect rest, never to allow himself to drop his guard. He is always in strange country, never sure of his way, never able to relax and sleep. Every night he and his squadron ride about in circles looking for the regiment. If they find it, they spend the rest of the night doing chores. They are constantly moving, both under orders and to escape enemy fire. Because they never know where they are, all movement is equally valid; if they happen to reach what they are looking for, it is completely by accident. Fear of the enemy and of authorities teaches him always to flee, or imagine he is fleeing, never knowing if it is from a danger or toward a shelter. In fact, he will eventually discover that it is neither: the danger is everywhere and the concept of shelter illusory. Still, having seen his colonel blown to bits standing "smack in the middle of the road," (V, 16) Bardamu finds it safest to run, with or without a destination.

Most of his movement takes place at night, a dangerous time. Looking back on his life, the narrator will see it all as a journey through night. It is partly because of the darkness that he sees so many walls around him. At first he sees the night as threatening: "une nuit énorme qui bouffait la route à deux pas de nous et même qu'il n'en sortait du noir qu'un petit bout de route grand comme la langue" (V, 26: "an enormous night that swallowed the road a few steps in front of us and in fact all that stuck out of the dark was a little bit of road as big as your tongue").

Later Bardamu learns that the night helps him to hide, and later narrators show an affinity for night. Many of the major incidents in Guignol's Band and Nord are enacted at night, and almost all of Normance takes place in the space of a single night. It is not, according to Bardamu, that night is so friendly, but rather that the day is so hostile: "La nuit, dont on avait eu si peur dans les premiers temps, en devenait par comparaison assez douce" (V, 36: "Nighttime, which we were so afraid of at first, became by comparison fairly pleasant").

Finally, Bardamu determines to explore the night, to throw himself into it and allow himself to be devoured by it in order to come to know it. He experiences war, poverty, and ill health; he dabbles in crime, and at last he finds, not that he has taken everything from the night, but that the night has taken everything from him: "Elle a tout pris la nuit et les regards eux-mêmes. On est vidé par elle" (V, 335: "The night has taken everything, even the power of sight. It empties you out").

After the war he leaves Europe for Africa, only to find the jungle, where movement is limited to a tunnel chopped out on the spot, "à la manière des rats dans les bottes de foin" (V, 161: "like rats in a haystack"), or taking to the river and paddling upstream, Bardamu's choice. Although his behavior in the labyrinth might very appropriately be compared to that of a rat, he refuses the name. Bardamu is still learning about the structure of his environment; he believes his movement has a purpose. Later he will recognize that his flight is motivated by the very structure of his space: because he is in the labyrinth, he must keep moving.

This is what he will do in the halls of the Hotel Laugh Calvin, when he arrives in New York. Again he is in strange territory--an American hotel--and he has no time to look about, "C'est aller qu'il faut, je m'en rends bien compte" (V, 197: "I have to keep moving, I'm aware of that"). The hotel is constructed very much like the châteaux the doctor of Nord finds in Germany, the hospital in Guignol's Band, and the prison from which Féerie is written. Each of these structures is a prison of sorts--a prison in which the attempt to escape is part of the code. The writing of Féerie is the only escape possible for the true prisoner, and he too finds that one labyrinth leads to another, that in writing, he forges himself a tunnel--makes of a sentence a path to follow--that he hesitates at each crossroads in choosing his words, that he is caught up in the movement of an "emotional metro." His novel is a verbal labyrinth.

Having learned the need for constant movement, Céline's narrators further discover that all motion is dangerous. At war Bardamu realizes that he is just as likely to stumble upon a French sentry who will shoot him by mistake as a German who will kill him by design. In Nord, Lili and the cat are almost shot for taking an evening stroll in the Reichsgesundt. Because Bardamu's sense of space is formed by the war, this pervasive atmosphere of paranoia continues throughout the novel, even in a hotel during peacetime.

> On essaye de ne pas se faire trop remarquer à l'hôtel. Ça ne vaut rien. Déjà dès qu'on s'engueule un peu fort ou trop souvent, ça va mal, on est repéré. A la fin on ose à peine pisser dans le lavabo, tellement que tout s'entend d'une chambre à l'autre. (V, 350)

> (You try not to be too conspicuous in a hotel. It doesn't work. As soon as you start arguing a little too loudly or too often, that does it, you're spotted. In the end you hardly dare piss in the sink, everything is so audible from one room to the next.)

Bardamu finds himself in a similar predicament on board the Amiral Bragueton. Fear of his fellow passengers confines him to his cabin. He literally imprisons himself. His natural functions take on disproportionate significance; his inability to perform them in the prescribed manner emphasizes his alienation from his fellows. As an outcast, he is unable to adhere to the accepted canon of behavior:

> il me devenait franchement périlleux de me rendre aux cabinets. Quand nous n'eûmes donc plus que ces trois jours de mer devant nous, j'en profitai pour définitivement renoncer à tous mes besoins naturels. Les hublots me suffisaient. (V, 118)
>
> (it was becoming downright dangerous to go to the toilet. So when we had just those three days left at sea, I took the opportunity to renounce the claims of my bodily needs. The portholes sufficed.)

Bardamu reverts to subhuman, animal-like behavior by relieving himself through the porthole. His change in toilet habits is not likely to go unnoticed. Instead of becoming less conspicuous, he is calling attention to himself as one who adopts peculiar manners of disposing of his bodily waste.

As Bardamu has discovered, movement can be just as dangerous as standing still. No movement is unobserved, for one is always being spied upon--at home, at the front, abroad. When he is wounded and sent to the hospital, he is still unable to drop his guard. In the hospital there are no secrets. An indiscretion will be punished by death just as surely as a false move in battle. He can have confidence in no one, certainly not in his sexual partner, the concierge, who sells her favors to the officers only to repeat everything they tell her to the head doctor. Here the concierge, traditionally a spy, is also a prostitute, transformed into a petty Delilah whose treachery is repeated on a daily basis.

In the Brenner Hotel in Baden-Baden the narrator of <u>Nord</u>
defines the relationships between the guests as a constant
spying and telling of tales.

> Bien entendu la Bibici, Brazzaville et la
> Chaux-de-Fonds étaient renseignés avant nous
> des moindres variations d'humeur, des plus
> minimes glouglous de bidets . . . vous pou-
> viez entendre heure par heure tous les haut-
> parleurs des couloirs sonner toutes les sta-
> tions du monde et toutes les nouvelles du
> «Brenner» . . . vous appreniez par Trébizonde
> ce qui se passait la chambre à côté [...]
> c'est un fait, personne ira oser prétendre
> qu'il y avait quelque chose de caché au
> «Brenner Hotel» . . . (<u>Nord</u>, 307-308)

> (Naturally the Beebeesee, Brazzaville and
> Chaux-de-Fonds were informed before we were
> of the slightest changes in mood, of the ti-
> niest gurglings in the bidets . . . you could
> hear hour by hour all the loudspeakers in the
> halls blaring out all the stations in the
> world and all the news of the "Brenner" . . .
> you learned from Trebizond what was going on
> in the room next door [...] it's a fact, no
> one would dare try to maintain there was any-
> thing hidden at the "Brenner Hotel" . . .)

As before, the lack of privacy is demonstrated by a reference
to the plumbing. The pipes supporting the toilets, sinks,
and bidets so often mentioned do in fact form a hidden labyrinth whose workings, although secret, are essential to the
well-being of the group. The doctor suggests that this un-
derlying network is of greater importance to the people
around him than any visible, tangible organization of space
previously encountered. Bardamu's recognition that he must
confine himself to his cabin and openly renounce his right to
utilize the public plumbing labyrinth is the imaginative

equivalent of retiring to a cloistered life of the mind, leaving lesser concerns to lesser intellects. The doctor is also announcing his superiority when he points out that the major concern of the spying in the Brenner is the functioning of the bidets.

This atmosphere of spying pervades the entire novel and allusions to it form a refrain at every change of residence. In Berlin the man across the street mysteriously comes into possession of a fan Lili had been keeping in her suitcase. In the _Reichsgesundt_ the doctor tries to dispose of a compromising weapon by dropping it in the Finnish pool, but it is found again almost immediately. At Zornhof, well, "pas de secrets possibles à Zornhof!" (_Nord_, 485: "no secrets possible at Zornhof!"). Not only is everyone aware that the doctor takes cigarettes and food from a wardrobe to which Harras has given him the key, but they all know better than he the contents of the secret wardrobe. He finds himself being told by two farm workers how to open the false bottom to find the liquor.

The doctor is convinced that the reason everyone is spying on him is that they all want to kill him. Once again his solution is to isolate himself from others and fulfill his needs in unconventional ways (by helping himself from the mysterious, almost magical chest). And once again his attempt to make himself inconspicuous has exactly the opposite effect.

The doctor's flamboyant efforts to keep out of sight
continue in the later novels. In Normance he hides even from
his friend Ottavio in case he has become as crazy as the other people in the apartment building:

> . . . peut-être qu'il était devenu dingue,
> vicieux, étripeur, comme les autres? . . .
> oh, gafe! . . . gafe! . . . gafe! . . . que
> je me recroqueville encore plus! . . . d'un
> bras, sous le tas, sous les plâtras, je racle
> . . . je ramène . . . je m'accumule plein de
> caillots! . . . plein la figure . . . je m'en
> barbouille . . . et d'ordures aussi! . . . il
> s'agit que je me camoufle . . . (N, 305)

> (. . . maybe he had gone crazy, vicious,
> butcher like the rest? . . . oh, watch it! .
> . . watch it! . . . watch it! I need to curl
> up even smaller! . . . with one arm, under
> the heap, under the debris, I rake . . . I
> sweep . . . I cover myself with clots! . . .
> all over my face . . . I smear myself . . .
> and with garbage too! . . . I'm camouflaging
> myself . . .)

The doctor believes that covering himself with garbage is an
effective camouflage. This reveals both his disdain for his
neighbors and his obsession with waste material. He adopts
immobility and protective covering (garbage) to blend in with
his surroundings and escape notice.

Above all, as the narrator eventually learns, the unpardonable infraction in this world is the one thing he can
scarcely control: change. Whether he moves or refrains from
moving, he must not allow his appearance, habits, or beliefs
to exhibit change. In Guignol's Band all the characters are
engaged in some form of illegal activity of which the police
are perfectly aware. The officers, properly paid off or sim-

ply indifferent, have elected to tolerate these breaches of the law; what they will not tolerate is any unannounced change in the routine to which they have become accustomed. An opium-dealer who has never had any problems with the police is suddenly on their wanted list when the war forces her to change to hashish. "C'est ça que le yard pardonnait pas, les variations des habitudes!" (G-B, 114: "That's what the Yard couldn't forgive, changing habits!"). Ferdinand illustrates this point with a particularly ridiculous example. He observes in a pub that Inspector Matthew feels personally offended by Borokrom's change of hat and is determined to punish the offense:

> Il en restait interloqué comme ça tout flan le sergent Matthew du nouveau chapeau de son homme. Ça lui coupait net son sifflet . . . Ça lui figeait son sourire. Il en croyait pas ses yeux! [...] Il se met à injurier l'artiste . . . (G-B, 35)
>
> (It knocked Sergeant Matthew speechless, flat out, his man's new hat. It cut off his wind . . . froze his smile. He couldn't believe his eyes! [...] He starts insulting the artiste . . .)

Borokrom is not reproached for anything illegal or even significant; he has merely made himself conspicuous when he was expected to blend in with the crowd. Conformity is the order of the day. Refusing to accept the slightest change on the part of others is the ultimate reification. Theseus hunted through the halls of the labyrinth, denied rest, privacy, freedom of movement, and the simple pleasure of changing his

hat, is no longer the hero of the past; he is not even a dig-
nified human being. His view of the world is so distorted he
believes the best camouflage is garbage.

Madelon shoots Robinson at the end of Voyage for aban-
doning her, for disdaining her love, but also for changing,
for loving her and then becoming indifferent to love. "Mais
dites-le donc tous que vous voulez changer! . . . Avouez-le!
. . . Que c'est du nouveau qu'il vous faut!" (V, 482: "Go
ahead and say it, that you all want to change! . . . Admit
it! . . . You need something new!") This is the reproach she
flings at Robinson and Bardamu. Certainly Bardamu left Molly
because he needed change; Robinson chooses to die because he
has exhausted the possibilities of life; its values leave him
indifferent, and dying is the only new experience remaining
for him. There are no resources for renewal in the labyrinth; any change must lead to death. The effects of time
are inescapable and unpardonable.

Life for Céline's narrators is motivated by fear: fear
makes them flee, fear makes them hide. They are punished for
existing--for moving, not moving, changing. Their problem is
not so much the experience of the tragic paradox as their lucid perception of it: "Lucid pain: this is the nihilistic
version of the traditional tragic argument that suffering
brings wisdom."[8] What suffering brings to the narrators is
the necessity for self-expression. The sense of persecution
is inherent in their structure of space, the labyrinth; the

need to describe the experience is part of their attempt to escape.

Many Monsters

Although the day may be delayed, at some point in the labyrinth one is expected to meet the monster. For any but a super-hero, this should be the end of the journey. The road may be long, and it may seem never-ending, but somewhere between the walls lurks the Minotaur. This is so inevitable that a sense of the monster's presence pervades every corner of confusing, branching space. It looms like the knowledge of mortality in the protagonist's mind.

Death is ever-present in the labyrinth. Its odor is everywhere. One of the principal characteristics of city streets and hospitals is their odor, recalling garbage and rotting matter on the one hand, illness and death on the other. In the streets: "Il y a des usines qu'on évite en se promenant, qui sentent toutes les odeurs, les unes à peine croyables et où l'air d'alentour se refuse à puer davantage" (V, 95: "There are factories you avoid when out walking, they combine every smell, some of them scarcely believable, and the air around them can't stink any further"). The direction of movement is thus influenced by greater and lesser stinks; Bardamu turns away from the more noxious ones as from a confrontation with death.

The very walls of the passages around him remind Bardamu of death. He sees them as caskets, as symbols of his unfulfilled possibilities.

> Par terre, la boue vous tire sur la fatigue
> et les côtés de l'existence sont fermés aus-
> si, bien clos par des hôtels et des usines
> encore. C'est déjà des cercueils les murs de
> ce côté-là. (V, 95)

> (Underfoot, the mud drags on your fatigue and
> the edges of existence are closed off too,
> well walled up by hotels and more factories.
> The walls in that part of town are already
> caskets.)

Bardamu imagines himself moving through a giant tomb, like an Egyptian pyramid. His future is, in effect, a monument to his past. He is thus constructing the labyrinth by his very existence; every failed opportunity erects another wall. He will eventually totally immure himself; he is his own execu- tioner. Although Sartre condemned Céline's anti-Semitic works, he admired Voyage and was strongly influenced by his verbal realism. In fact, the epigraph to La Nausée is a quote from L'Eglise. In La Nausée we find a passage similar to the one above:

> Devant le passage Gillet, je ne sais plus que
> faire. Est-ce qu'on ne m'attend pas au fond
> du passage? Mais il y a aussi, place Duco-
> ton, au bout de la rue Tournebride, une cer-
> taine chose qui a besoin de moi pour naître.
> Je suis plein d'angoisse: le moindre geste
> m'engage. Je ne peux deviner ce qu'on veut
> de moi. Il faut pourtant choisir: je sacri-
> fie le passage Gillet, j'ignorerai toujours
> ce qu'il me réservait.[9]

> (Before the Passage Gillet I don't know what
> to do. Am I not expected at the end of the
> passage? But there is also, in the Place Du-
> coton, at the end of the Rue Tournebride, a
> certain something that needs my presence to
> come to life. I am filled with anguish: the
> slightest gesture commits me. I cannot guess

what is wanted of me. Yet I must choose: I
sacrifice the Passage Gillet, I will never
know what it held in store for me.)

In each case the protagonist is reminded by the walls around
him that he has committed himself to a path, thus closing off
all the other paths he might have taken: "les côtés de
l'existence sont fermés" (V, 95: "the edges of existence are
closed off"). Once he has chosen, something has been "sacri-
ficed," and the walls that close in after each decision--each
sacrifice of something within himself--are the instruments of
his immolation. The labyrinth comes into being around him;
he himself is responsible.

The self-made labyrinth, constructed by the writer as
his own tomb, is at once a metaphor for life, the novel, and
the body. The traditional poetic image of a person feeling
himself to be imprisoned within his body is given new breadth
when the body becomes more than a prison cell; it is a complex system of winding tunnels, an anatomist's view blown up
to world size. Céline's narrators, as doctors, always accept
the body as a finite biological fact; this does not prevent
them from struggling to escape its confinement. Their obses-
sive narration, particularly in Féerie pour une autre fois,
is a sustained effort to reach beyond their own physical lim-
its, to break the bonds of human isolation, to perpetuate
themselves in their story.

They do indeed succeed in reaching beyond their own
boundaries into a larger world, a world that is but a larger-

scale representation of themselves. Bardamu is a self-contained labyrinth lost in the labyrinthine innards of a giant beast. This is particularly clear in the delineation and characterization of the city.

The city in Voyage, as Schilling has noted, is a labyrinth in which the hero is surrounded by monsters.[10] This is certainly true of New York, of which Bardamu says,

> . . . pour moi ce n'était rien qu'un abominable système de contraintes, en briques, en couloirs, en verrous, en guichets, une torture architecturale gigantesque, inexpiable. (V, 205)
>
> (. . . in my opinion it was just an abominable network of restraints, made of bricks, of hallways, of lock bolts, of wickets, a gigantic architectural torture, inexpiable.)

Here the city is compared to the underground torture chamber and prison complex of a medieval castle. Bardamu feels restrained; his freedom of movement is curtailed by the bolts, bricks, and hallways. Because he cannot move freely, he calls the city an "architectural torture."

The city appears as a labyrinthine structure in many modern novels--for example, Michel Butor's L'Emploi du temps, where every page attests to Revel's struggle against time, and, on the last page, his ultimate defeat. Time is not the only adversary in this novel: John J. White suggests that "the city itself is both maze and minotaur."[11] Like Balzac, who personifies Paris at the end of Le Père Goriot with Rastignac's defiant "A nous deux maintenant!" ("Now it's

between the two of us!"), Céline, with his description of New
York as a "city standing up," makes of the city a character:

> Mais chez nous, n'est-ce pas, elles sont cou-
> chées les villes, au bord de la mer ou sur
> les fleuves, elles s'allongent sur le pay-
> sage, elles attendent le voyageur, tandis que
> celle-là l'Américaine elle ne se pâmait pas,
> non elle se tenait bien raide, là, pas bai-
> sante du tout, raide à faire peur. (V, 184)

> (But where we come from you know, the cities
> are reclining, at the seashore or on the riv-
> ers, they stretch out on the landscape, they
> await the traveler, whereas this American one
> wasn't swooning, no it was good and stiff
> standing there, not at all a turn-on, stiff
> enough to scare you.)

The city is an antagonist, and in this case the monster is
not inside the labyrinth; the labyrinth is inside the monster. The maze of city streets forms a labyrinth within the
city, and people are insignificant beasts struggling to sur-
vive in the entrails of a leviathan.

The labyrinth is thus another adversary. There is no
exit but death, no possibility of victory for the victim.
One escapes from the war to the hospital, from the town to
the forest, from hotel to street; there is no escape from the
labyrinth. Everywhere the same baffling space stretches its
tentacles on every side. Bardamu confronts the surrounding
space and recognizes that he is losing the battle.

Céline succeeds in portraying a labyrinthine world
filled with monsters on a mythological scale: death, the
self, the city, and the labyrinth itself are all descendants
of the Minotaur.

Girl Scouts

A thread led Theseus out of the labyrinth, and at the end of the thread stood Ariadne. There is some disagreement among critics about the role of women in Céline's work. Some find women relatively important, but not love.[12] Some feel that Lola's body holds a truth;[13] some even see a theme of rebirth through the woman-dancer.[14] Although Céline uses the term "erotico-mysticism" in Voyage to describe a sense of exaltation brought on by a combination of hunger and sex deprivation, his remarks about women are generally no less disparaging than his remarks about men, and the occasional passages in Voyage extolling sexual union--which alternate with such disdainful statements as "L'amour c'est l'infini mis à la portée des caniches" (V, 12: "Love is the infinite within the reach of poodles")--entirely disappear from the later works.

With few exceptions, Céline deals with only two types of women: dancers and prostitutes. Scarcely a female figure is not promiscuous at the very least, while Lola, Musyne, and Molly, in Voyage, Cascade's bevy in Guignol's Band, and the fleeing pack of women in Nord all openly practice prostitution. The dancers include Tania and her English companions in Voyage, Lili and the gypsies in Nord. Both types of women may be guides to a sensual experience with possibilities for transcendence. However, orgasm is a deceptive and fleeting

pleasure; dance suggests mystery without unveiling any secrets. The most extensive treatment of the sexual experience
is in Voyage. The later novels reject not only the transcen-
dent power of orgasm, but any pleasure in the female not associated with healthy muscles and graceful dancing. Women do
seem to possess some secret power, a power not related to the
intellect, for they are generally an unreflective lot, and
they are unable--or unwilling--to communicate their secret.

Throughout Voyage Bardamu looks to women for directions
through the labyrinth. Lola brings him a new vision: "Je
reçus ainsi tout près du derrière de Lola le message d'un
nouveau monde" (V, 55: "Thus it was from right around Lola's
rear end that I received the message of a new world"). This
message leads him to America, land of beautiful women. In
fact, he finds what he is looking for in the streets of New
York. Awestruck by the beauty of the women streaming by, he
says, "Je touchais au vif de mon pélérinage" (V, 193: "I
was reaching the goal of my pilgrimage"). He is suggesting
that women are more than guides, that they are the end itself, that in sexual titillation he removes himself from time
and the physical body, finds his religion. He is particularly impressed by the women's disdain for him, by the impossi-
bility of communicating with them. Because his perceptions
are already distorted by fever, quinine, and hunger, the
whole episode has the quality of a hallucination, with aloof
untouchable women streaming endlessly by.

> Elles me parurent d'autant mieux divines ces
> apparitions, qu'elles ne semblaient point du
> tout s'apercevoir que j'existais, moi, là, à
> côté sur ce banc, tout gâteux, baveux d'admi-
> ration érotico-mystique de quinine et aussi
> de faim, faut l'avouer. S'il était possible
> de sortir de sa peau j'en serais sorti juste
> à ce moment-là, une fois pour toutes. Rien
> ne m'y retenait plus. (V, 193-194)

> (They seemed all the more divine to me these
> apparitions, for not appearing to notice my
> existence, me, right there on the bench, go-
> ing gaga, drooling with erotico-mystical ad-
> miration from quinine and hunger as well, I
> must admit. If it were possible to leave
> one's skin I would have left it right at that
> moment, once and for all. Nothing was hold-
> ing me back.)

Although "nothing" restrains him, Bardamu does not soar out
of his skin, even in fancy. The ecstasy he feels in contem-
plating female bodies is belied by his experience of sexual
intercourse.

The glimpse of the infinite that orgasm provides is particularly frustrating because it opens onto a vast lonely
plain of endless unquenchable thirst.

> On peut baiser tout ça. C'est bien agréable
> de toucher ce moment où la matière devient la
> vie. On monte jusqu'à la plaine infinie qui
> s'ouvre devant les hommes. On en fait: ouf!
> Et ouf! On jouit tant qu'on peut dessus et
> c'est comme un grand désert . . . (V, 464)

> (All that is worth balling. It's great to
> touch the moment matter becomes life. You
> climb up to the infinite plain which spreads
> out before men. You go, oof, and again oof!
> You come as hard as you can on top and it's
> like one big desert . . .)

The customary euphemistic love language is replaced by a naturalistic sound designating relief, leaving the reader with the feeling that one descends, rather than rises, to the infinite plain.

A pleasure that promises less deception is the purely visual enjoyment of female beauty. In <u>Voyage</u> Bardamu derives considerable pleasure from looking at women, in the passage cited about New York, and again when he praises Sophie's body, just before the above description of orgasm.

> Pour mon compte et pour tout dire, je n'en finissait plus de l'admirer. De muscles en muscles, par groupes anatomiques, je procédais . . . Par versants musculaires, par régions . . . Cette vigueur concertée mais déliée en même temps, répartie en faisceaux fuyants et consentants tour à tour, au palper, je ne pouvais me lasser de la poursuivre . . . Sous la peau veloutée, tendue, détendue, miraculeuse . . .
> L'ère de ces joies vivantes, des grandes harmonies indéniables, physiologiques, comparatives est encore à venir . . . Le corps, une divinité tripotée par mes mains honteuses . . . (<u>V</u>, 462)

> (As for me, to be frank, I couldn't admire her enough. From muscle to muscle, by anatomical groups, I proceeded . . . By muscular slopes, by regions . . . I never wearied of pursuing this vigor, bunched but unbound, in clusters fleeing or yielding to the touch by turns . . . Beneath the skin so velvety, taut, lax, miraculous . . .
> The age of these living joys, of great undeniable harmonies, physiological and comparative, is still to come . . . The body, a divinity sullied by my shameful hands . . .)

After pouring out this flow of words in praise of Sophie's body and specifically equating "body" with "divinity," Bardamu rejects the idea that there is anything sacred in the act of love. "C'est barbouillé d'une crasse épaisse de symboles, et capitonné jusqu'au trognon d'excréments artistiques que l'homme distingué va tirer son coup . . . " (V, 462: "The man of distinction has to be smeared with a thick coating of symbols and padded to the butthole with artistic excrement to get his rocks off"). Bardamu is a sexually active man, but the pleasure he derives from sex is minimal; he enjoys looking at beautiful women more than touching them. In any case the older doctor in Nord has rigorous standards of beauty, and he suggests that beauty contests be judged in the same honest and healthy manner that animals are judged.

The divorce of pleasure from physical sensation inspires in the narrator a passionate love of dance. His admiration for female grace in movement replaces, in the later novels, the earlier appreciation of women "made for love." The doctor's wife Lili, his companion in Normance and Nord, is an almost mute creature with a special ability to communicate with animals. Saving their skins has become the doctor's goal, and he no longer expresses any interest in women other than an impersonal admiration for the graceful movements of a healthy trained dancer:

> au vrai, je regarde plus les femmes depuis des années . . . l'âge sans doute, et puis aussi les événements . . . quand la forêt brûle les plus loustics animaux et les plus féroces pensent plus ni aux bagatelles ni à se dévorer . . . (Nord, 477)

> (actually, I haven't looked at a woman in
> years . . . must be getting old, and with all
> the upheavals . . . when the forest is burn-
> ing even the horniest and most ferocious ani-
> mals quit thinking about getting it on to-
> gether or eating each other up . . .)

Dance, for the spectator, is love-making with the eye. It is a more intimate experience than voyeurism because no third person intervenes. It is a cerebral pleasure based on a celebration of the physical body. The distance it demands between dancer and spectator make it a wholly intangible experience. The person watching, in this case male, does not participate in the action, and he concludes that the woman enjoys a power that he can never know. It is impossible for him to form a precise idea of her secret, but he believes all women to share it. Furthermore, the dance is dangerous because it makes one want to die:

> Ça commençait d'un petit ton gentil leur
> chanson, ça n'avait l'air de rien, comme
> toutes les choses pour danser, et puis voilà
> que ça vous faisait pencher le coeur à force
> de vous faire triste comme si on allait per-
> dre à l'entendre l'envie de vivre (V, 357).
>
> (Their song started out on light note, it
> didn't seem like much of anything, like all
> dance tunes, and then all at once it plucked
> at your heartstrings, it made you feel so
> sad, as if on hearing it you were about to
> lose your will to live).

As they dance, the Englishwomen of the Tarapout sing a siren song.

The terms "dance" and "death" are easily linked, and the danse macabre theme is discernable in all Céline's novels, where both death and dancers hold such a large place. It is with Tania that Bardamu has his gory angel hallucination where all the dead people he has known parade by in the clouds, and the nearby cemeteries empty their ghosts into the sky (V, 359-361). It is while the gypsies dance in Nord that the von Leiden son and the Landrat are murdered. In Normance Mimi dances with Jules on the windmill above the burning city. Gustave's "Dance of the Fire" at the end of Voyage is a final reminder that death leads us dancing to the grave.

It is possible for writing to imitate dance in its graceful, fluid motion. Allen Thiher remarks that parts of Guignol's Band are a linguistic dance.[15] The spectator then is the reader, who follows with his eye the graceful movement of the sentence. His pleasure is based on a visual grasp of rhythm, narrative pace, direct and twisting lines of thought, and the music of his own sub-vocalization of the text. Reading may be less disappointing than dance because the written word does not strive to be ineffable.

The crucial moment in the Theseus-Ariadne love affair is Theseus' desertion of Ariadne. Even Jacques Revel in L'Emploi du temps finds the pattern of abandonment being completed against his will. Although Bardamu asserts in his erotic ecstasy in New York his readiness to follow women anywhere, although he actually went to America because of Lola, he in fact abandons every single woman of his acquaintance, beginning with his mother, and for none of them will he deviate from the path he has chosen for himself. He will not become a hero, as Lola advises him, he does not follow Musyne even so far as the butcher's cellar, Molly he abandons outright, even though she is supporting him. It is ironic that he insists, "Elles n'avaient qu'un geste à faire . . . mais sans doute avaient-elles d'autres missions" (V, 194: "They had but to beckon . . . but they probably had other things to do"), that they are neglecting him.

He has no doubts about his destination, were he to choose to follow the indications women have given him. They point the road to death.

> Elles demeuraient décidément les garces du bon côté de la situation où régnait une consigne souriante mais implacable d'élimination envers nous autres, nous les viandes destinées aux sacrifices. (V, 96-97)

> (The bitches were certainly staying on the right side of a situation where reigned the smiling but implacable order for our elimination, us meat on the way to be sacrificed.)

Lola wanted Bardamu to return to battle, to almost certain death. Isis von Leiden tries to persuade the doctor to procure poisons for her--obviously, he thinks, in order to incriminate him, whether or not she is planning a murder. Delphine supplies the drugs which Ferdinand and Borokrom smoke before killing Claben, and it is the jilted Madelon who shoots Robinson. In short, women are dangerous.

Céline still sees in women some saving grace, a grace which saves them, if not others. Lili spent part of the night on the roof during the bombardment of Normance. She

returns in better shape than any of the tenants who had cow-
ered under the table below. She leaps down through the ceiling ("such grace! such grace!"), and the doctor describes
her survival as a miracle. "Mais les flammes alors? . . . et
les shrapnels? et les tornades dis, des avions? . . . elle
avait tout vu sur le toit!" (<u>N</u>, 313: "What about the
flames? . . . and the shrapnel? and the tornadoes of the
airplanes? . . . she saw it all on the roof!")

Indeed, women seem to have a special instinct for escaping the labyrinth. La Joconde, hospitalized for a knife-
wound in <u>Guignol's Band</u>, reappears unexpectedly in a bar, and
Cascade complains,

> Monsieur le Docteur Clodovitz! Je vous con-
> fie une personne blessée! Je la remets à vos
> bons soins! . . . Je crois qu'elle va se te-
> nir tranquille! . . . Je paye l'hôpital! Je
> paye tout! Je vous bourre de ronds joli doc-
> teur! C'est comme ça votre reconnaissance?
> Dites-moi un petit peu! . . . Ça se sauve
> comme ça veut de chez vous! (<u>G-B</u>, 129)

> (Dr. Clodovitz! I entrust a wounded person
> to you! I leave her in your care! . . . I
> expect her to stay put! . . . I pay for the
> hospital! I pay for everything! I shower
> you with cash my fine doctor! And this is
> the thanks I get? I ask you now! . . . They
> walk out whenever they please at your place!)

In fact, the narrator of <u>D'un château l'autre</u> tells us in so
many words that women have an instinct for finding their way
through mazes: "les femmes ont l'instinct des dédales, des
torts et travers, elles s'y retrouvent . . . le sens animal!"[16] ("women have a feeling for mazes, for twists and

turns, they come into their own . . . it's animal instinct!").

Men cannot benefit from this instinct that women have because women are not to be trusted. The concierge who sold her favors to the soldiers and repeated their secrets to the head doctor is the very type of the woman as traitress. Worse--the city, a form of Minotaur, is unquestionably female: cities are either "reclining" and "awaiting the traveler," or, like New York, "not at all a turn-on." Women are beautiful to look at, dangerous to touch. They have some secret knowledge to save themselves and they will do just that, save themselves, with no regard for men but to betray them. They are graceful, they dance, but their dance is another version of Salome's dance for the head of John the Baptist.

The myth of the labyrinth, once a proud affirmation of man's supremacy where super-hero slaughters monster, wins woman, and later tosses her aside, has become for Céline a nightmare in which man is hunted from one street corner to the next, where the beautiful damsel withholds the thread and points the wrong way to the exit.

Man is the quarry in Céline's world, and he feels all the more anguish for knowing that the path he takes is of his own choosing. He is tormented by the double-bind: he must neither rest nor run, for either course of action will lead to death, and he must never change. He encounters many monsters, all impossible to elude, all bent on his destruction.

He looks to women, whose beauty affords him so much pleasure, for directions, but women direct him falsely, saving the truth for themselves.

The labyrinth is also a metaphor for the intestines, as we see when Bardamu explores the streets around the hospital.

> Dans le grand abandon mou qui entoure la ville, là où le mensonge de son luxe vient suinter et finir en pourriture, la ville montre à qui veut le voir son grand derrière en boîte à ordures. (V, 94-95)

> (In the great slack abandonment that surrounds the city, where the lie of its luxury comes to ooze and end up rotting, the city shows anybody who wants to see it her great rear end like a garbage can.)

Bardamu believes he is exploring the entrails of the monster city, examining her "great rear end" (we have already seen the city as a reclining slut awaiting the traveler). He expects to learn something from these entrails, as if he were a priest performing a divinatory rite on a steaming heap of sacrificial guts. Following this intestinal path may lead somewhere. The protagonist consciously adopts this route to find out where it leads and what thing of value may lie at its end. Both Gaston Bachelard and Gilbert Durand mention that the labyrinth is the entrance to hell.[17] The questing hero descends a tortuous path to reach the underground. What he finds there remains to be seen.

Notes

[1]"Rat pris au piège." Gilbert Schilling, "Espace et angoisse dans _Voyage au bout de la nuit_," _Revue des Lettres Modernes_, No. 398-402 (1974), 67-68.

[2]Gaston Bachelard, _La Terre et les rêveries du repos_ (Paris: José Corti, 1948), p. 213. For Bachelard, the two "angoisses" of the labyrinth are narrowness and choice.

[3]Angus Fletcher, _The Prophetic Moment_ (Chicago: Univ. of Chicago Press, 1971), p. 29.

[4]_Plutarch's Lives, the Dryden Plutarch_ rev. by Arthur Hugh Clough (New York: E. P. Dutton, 1910), vol. 1, p. 11.

[5]Alain Robbe-Grillet, _Dans le labyrinthe_ (Paris: Minuit, 1959). André Gide, _Thésée_ (Paris: Gallimard, 1949). Albert Camus, _Le Minotaure_ (Paris: Charlot, 1950).

[6]P. S. Day, _Le Miroir allégorique de L.-F. Céline_ (Paris: Klincksieck, 1974), p. 231.

[7]Jean-Pierre Richard, _Nausée de Céline_ (Paris: Fata Morgana, 1973), pp. 80-82.

[8]Kingsley Widmer, "The Way Down to Wisdom of Louis-Ferdinand Céline," _Minnesota Review_, 8 (1968), p. 88.

[9]Jean-Paul Sartre, _La Nausée_ (Paris: Gallimard, 1938), p. 76.

[10]Schilling, p. 68.

[11]John J. White, _Mythology in the Modern Novel_ (Princeton: Princeton Univ. Press, 1971), p. 213.

[12]Marc Hanrez, _Céline_ (Paris: Gallimard, 1961), p. 275. Albert Chesneau points out in his _Essai de psychocritique de L.-F. Céline_ (Archives des Lettres Modernes, No. 129, 1971), p. 72, that the almost total absence of the theme of love is unique. As Marcel Bataillon remarks in _Le Roman picaresque_ (Paris: La Renaissance du Livre, 1931), love is a little-known character in the picaresque novel (p. 21).

[13]Philippe Alméras, "Du sexe au texte avec arrêt raciste," _Revue des Lettres Modernes_, No. 398-402 (1974), 81.

[14]Erika Ostrovsky, _Céline and His Vision_ (New York: NYU Press, 1967), p. 45.

[15]Allen Thiher, _Céline: The Novel as Delirium_ (New Brunswick, NJ: Rutgers Univ. Press, 1972), p. 107.

[16]Céline, _D'un château l'autre_ (Paris: Gallimard, 1957), p. 126.

[17]It is in _Aurélia_ that Bachelard sees the labyrinth as a descent into hell (op. cit., p. 231), and he suggests that in each person's "psychic house" there is a labyrinth leading to his/her private hell (p. 232). He uses the labyrinthine sewer of _Les Misérables_ as the example of the intestinal metaphor (pp. 250-251). Gilbert Durand speaks of the intestines as the entrance to hell in _Les Structures anthropologiques de l'imaginaire_ (Paris: Bordas, 1969), p. 132.

II

FALLS

Except for an isolated example of flight in _Normance_ (the Lutry family disappears into a hole in the sky), the balloon ascents in _Mort_ _à_ _crédit_, and occasional stair climbings in all the novels, ascent is almost absent from Céline's work, and it is certainly not a predominant theme. The spiritual connotations normally ascribed to rising have no place in Céline's world. Descent, on the other hand, is prevalent. In the vertical continuum, both climbing and flying may be performed in either direction and represent the two extremes of laborious and effortless movement. The most important distinction between upward and downward movement is that ascent is almost always a voluntary and controlled undertaking, whereas falling, one of the most common forms of descent in human experience, is rapid, involuntary, and uncontrolled. The closest rising counterpart is a strong upward draft, but this is not at all a satisfactory equivalent. Upward drafts of such force are rare, and the sensation of being sucked into the sky cannot be compared with the sensation of plummeting to earth. It is logically impossible to fall up.

Our stock of proverbs and idioms teaches us that descent is dangerous, humiliating, and unwise. "Look before you leap," "Pride goeth before a fall," "backing down," "he fell for it," are verbalizations of what is one of the first and strongest fears in humans, since falling is not only an instinctive fear in babies, associated with the birth trauma; it is also an inevitable, repeated proof of failure as the child passes from infantile to adult locomotion, from crawling to walking.[1] Similar expressions tell us that what is "higher" is better, and moving "up" is desirable. Heaven is situated somewhere in the sky, hell somewhere deep beneath the earth.

Falling is automatically, if only through homonymy, associated with the Fall, thus acquiring immediate moral connotations. The myth of the Fall from Eden, originally an explanation for temporality and death,[2] shows falling to lead to death, as is often the case in literature, for even Icarus was killed not by his flight but by his fall. Falling is thus both a humiliating act and a move toward death. Céline's protagonists turn their falls to advantage by describing what they find. They are looking for what lies under the labyrinth, and their search takes them in the direction of death.

Falling in literature does not by any means always result in death. The Wonderland motif--diving below the surface to a world which obeys different laws--is also to be found in Céline's novels. The fall into a dream world, which for Alice, as for most of us, was the plunge from the waking world into sleep, reveals a magic (or in some cases grotesque) underworld. The faller moves from one mode of existence to another. Normance, for example, is the story of the "féerie" discovered by the narrator when he fell down the elevator shaft. This may be delirium, as both Allen Thiher and Marie-Christine Bellosta suggest,[3] or it may be a novel-length nightmare. In either case the world of Normance belongs to the realm of dream, and the narration of Normance is the eventual result of the narrator's fall. Instead of falling into temporality, he falls out of it and into a nontemporal fantasy world.

Another, unusually extensive treatment of the theme of falling in the twentieth century is the long poem Altazor, by Chilean Vicente Huidobro, which announces near the beginning, "Altazor you will die," and follows the central figure, Altazor, in an endless fall which is life--on an individual, historical, and universal level.

> Cae de tu cabeza a tus pies
> Cae de tus pies a tu cabeza
> Cae del mar a la fuente
> Cae al último abismo de silencio
> Como el barco que se hunde apagando sus
>   luces[4]

```
(Fall from head to foot
 Fall from foot to head
 Fall from sea to fountain
 Fall to the last abyss of silence
 Like the sinking ship whose lights go out one
     by one)
```

Altazor falls into himself as well as into poetic space. His fall does not involve a change in modes of existence; it is in itself a mode of existence: "Fall eternally". To experience existence as an unending fall is not only to feel that life is without support of any kind, but also to fail to distinguish between the emptiness of life and the void after death. Céline makes a very clear distinction between daytime and nighttime, two very different forms of existence, with falling as the passage between them. Death too is a fall, this time into a mode of non-existence, the cessation of consciousness. There can be no further falling after death, since the sensation of emptiness is linked to consciousness. Death, the ultimate fall, must be an end.

Céline's narrators feel a compulsion to talk about what they see when they fall; the result is the novel. They describe the world they have fallen into, which is the world of dream.

Their falls often bring them close to death and imitate death-falls. In their nightmare worlds they may feel an urge to destroy themselves, but they live to repeat the experience, and to tell us that life is a repeated fall.

Murder is not uncommon in Céline's novels--the victim is usually pushed and falls to death. The pushing fulfills the murderer's (often momentary) desires and gives him the same power of control over his own existence as a writer has when he creates a literary world.

Wonderland

Endless, Altazor's fall is a constantly renewed terror, a fear not of an end, but of the infinite void. Céline's falls are not unending, nor even in some cases unproductive. The initial fall in _Normance_ was the inspiration for the novel; the entire hallucinatory narration was the result of the shock to the doctor's head when he fell down the elevator shaft. The doctor succeeded in moving from one mode of existence to another by falling; in this respect he entered a sort of "wonderland," with waltzing near-animate furniture, spectacular fireworks that change night into day, crevasses that appear and disappear seemingly at random.

The doctor thought he had fallen to his death: "le coup de l'ascenseur m'a fini! . . . je suis achevé . . . je me relèverai plus . . . " (_N_, 16: "this elevator business has finished me off! . . . I'm done for . . . I won't get up again . . . "). In fact, he is far from dead, but his perceptions are altered. Where others see an exploding bomb, he sees a sun rising in the west: "si vous aviez encore des yeux vous pourriez voir monter le soleil . . . un soleil qui surgit à l'ouest! . . . et tout magnésium!" (_N_, 130: "if you had any eyes left you could see the sun coming up . . . a sun springing up in the west! . . . all made of magnesium!"). He has fallen into a world which does not abide by familiar laws, where strange relationships abound. These incongruous associations are the essence of the poetic imagination.

Jules, the paraplegic painter, has appeared mysteriously at the top of a nearby windmill surrounded by flames. There is no explanation for his sudden appearance: "d'abord pourquoi il est là-haut? comment ils l'ont hissé? à bras? à dos? par poulies?" (N, 32: "why is he up there in the first place? how did they get him up there? in their arms? on their backs? with pulleys?"). The doctor suspects a practical joke, but he sees no evidence that anyone helped Jules scale the windmill. It is as if Jules and the doctor were attached to the opposite ends of a see-saw, so that when the doctor fell, Jules rose to the top of the windmill. Thus in the doctor's hallucinatory vision his fall initiated the bombardment, which Jules conducts like a symphony: "il orchestre tout! c'est lui qui oriente les foudres!" (N, 33: "He's orchestrating the whole thing! he's the one directing the lightning bolts!"), and Jules' fall will terminate it. Throughout the novel the doctor screams at Jules, "Jump! jump!" In a parody of the usual scene where the prospective suicide is begged not to jump, he taunts Jules, calls him a coward, and advises him to jump if he is thirsty.

Jules not only does not jump, he is later joined by Mimi, who climbs up the ladder, then knocks it down so that no one can pursue them. She immediately subdues Jules, slaps him, and dresses him like a doll. This scene on top of the windmill is the exact opposite of an earlier one (in Féerie

<u>pour</u> <u>une</u> <u>autre</u> <u>fois</u>) in which Jules seduced Lili in his base-
ment studio. As a distorted replay of an incident which was
traumatic to the doctor, it is characteristic of the world of
dream.

The doctor continues to fantasize a repetition of his
fall, by stumbling into the hole in the hall, or being sucked
into the elevator shaft, or being dropped by Ottavio carrying
him down the stairs. He behaves as if he had little control
over his movements—as if, in fact, he had no legs, like
Jules. During much of the novel he crawls or is carried, and
he certainly does not share Lili's freedom of movement.
There can be little doubt he has passed a mental pale; he has
fallen into a space of restricted movement which is distinct
from the conscious labyrinth.

The doctor feels compelled to describe the adventure he
stumbled into when he fell; he wants to write it down. At
the end of the novel the air is full of falling papers, pages
from his book: "avec ce qu'est tombé comme papiers! . . .
pensez, depuis des heures! . . . tornades sur tornades! . . .
l'épaisseur! . . . l'ensevelissement!" (<u>N</u>, 372: "with all
the papers that have fallen! . . . think of it, for hours on
end! . . . tornado after tornado! . . . so thick! . . . bury-
ing everything!"). The narrator's fall at the beginning, the
papers' fall at the end—one fall extends its influence forward, the other backward, and between them they form the novel. It is the reader, not the author, who must assemble the
fallen pages and create a coherent work. The narrator has

shown us a fall that catapulted him into another world; he has transcribed that confrontation with chaos and tossed us the fragments. He disclaims any responsibility (he was just on his way to the metro) and he leaves us with the pile of papers and his last words: "voilà les faits, exactement . . . " (N, 375: "those are the facts, exactly . . . "). If we choose to read this disorganized chronicle as a novel, it is up to us to impose a structure on it; part of the work of the novelist is left up to the reader.

Ferdinand of Guignol's Band also becomes a storyteller after falling. At one point he falls into a crowd of people and knocks over Sosthène. There are of course two points of view when a person falls on top of another: the one who fell will be "he who lost face" to himself and "he who appeared from the sky" to the other. Thus when Ferdinand is ejected from the French embassy and falls into the crowd outside the door, he immediately starts boasting to Sosthène, exaggerating his deeds out of all proportion. "J'en ai tué dix! . . . j'en ai tué mille! . . . je tombe du ciel!" (G-B, 259: "I've killed ten! . . . I've killed a thousand! . . . I fall from the sky!"). He wishes to erase his feeling of foolishness by portraying himself as a heroic figure--heroic in the old style, which still obtains in time of war, when the warrior is hero. He goes on to tell how he came to be in London, cutting short his recital with "Je peux pas tout vous dire d'un seul coup! . . . Moi qui vous tombe sur la tête!" (G-B, 263: "I can't tell you everything all at once! . . .

just falling on your head like that!"). The idiomatic meaning of "tomber du ciel"--to be a godsend--is of course used
to full advantage in this episode. Sosthène himself says,
"Vous tombez du ciel!" (G-B, 270: "You fall from the
sky!"). Both Sosthène and Ferdinand expect to profit from
this meeting. Certainly it is ironic that Ferdinand, wanted
for murder, mistrusted by his friends, who are pimps and murderers, rejected as unfit for military service, should be "he
who falls from the sky."

Ferdinand's adventures in London are as nightmarish as
the doctor's experiences in Paris, and the impetus to relate
them is also given by a fall. He sits down next to Sosthène
on the sidewalk and tells his story: "Je raconte mon histoire au Chinois, comme ça sur le rebord de pierre" (G-B,
262: "I'm telling my story to the Chinaman, right there on
the curb"). He describes his adventures in the "underworld"
of London, an underworld that could only be found in the
imagination. Ferdinand's story is not consistent; it is impossible to be certain how many people he has killed, why he
might have killed them, whether the Mille-Pattes murder is a
hallucination, or if the entire chaotic evening at Claben's
is merely a bad drug trip. We do know that the novel takes
place in a dream world and that Ferdinand's fall inspires him
to tell his history.

In both Normance and Guignol's Band, fallen narrators
relate their stories. The act of falling moves them into the
underworld and gives them the incentive to create a work of

fiction. The other world may be frightening, but it is fertile, since it gives birth to the novel. Northrop Frye points out that falling in romance is always linked to metamorphosis, which may be as simple as a change of name.[5] In these novels the fall explains how a character assumes the identity of narrator.

The Premature Burial

Other falls lead to less happy conclusions. Often the person who falls is covered by a weight or accidentally buried. These simulated burials are rehearsals for the death to come and may well be deliberate attempts to comprehend death before the fact. Existence provides many opportunities to practice falling, and the difference between the true performance and the dress rehearsal is that in life one must always get up and begin again.

Guignol's Band is introduced by a flight scene under fire along a road in France. A bridge collapsing leaves a hole in the pavement into which people fall.

> Les personnes fondent, tassent les crevasses!
> [...] L'on aperçoit un colonel, des Zouaves,
> je crois, qui se débat dans la cataracte . .
> . Il succombe sous le poids des morts! . . .
> bascule tout au fond . . . «Vive la France!»
> qu'il crie finalement . . . vaincu sous le
> tas des cadavres! (G-B, 17)

> (People are melting, filling in the breach!
> [...] A colonel can be seen, of the Zouaves,
> I think, thrashing around in the flood . . .
> He succumbs beneath the weight of the bodies!
> . . . knocked down to the bottom . . . "Vive
> la France!" he shouts at last . . . conquered
> by the pile of corpses!)

This scene prefigures the fall of Inspector Matthew in a bar:

> Basculé, raplati par terre, Matthew se trouve
> recouvert d'ivrognes, braillants, joyeux,
> trépignants dessus, en monticule jusqu'au
> lustre . . . caracolant d'aise et de vic-
> toire! La ronde aux godets passe dessus . .

. A sa santé . . . <u>For</u> <u>he</u> <u>is</u> <u>a</u> <u>jolly</u> <u>good</u>
<u>fellow</u>! (<u>G-B</u>, 36)

(Knocked down, flattened against the ground,
Matthew lies there covered with raucous, joy-
ous, trampling drunks, heaped up to the ceiling light . . . capering with delight and
victory! The toast goes round over his head
. . . To his health . . . <u>For</u> <u>he</u> <u>is</u> <u>a</u> <u>jolly</u>
<u>good</u> <u>fellow</u>!)

In both cases an unsympathetic character who represents the
forces of law and order falls under the weight of a number of
other people and a highly inappropriate popular expression
(Vive la France! For he is a jolly good fellow!) rounds off
with a chuckle an outrageously exaggerated banana-peel scene.

At another point Borokrom falls down the stairs in Claben's shop, knocking over a pile of dishes which bury a customer:

Il retitube . . . Broum! . . . il bascule
verse . . . débouline . . . croule dans la
boutique . . . Une masse . . . Comme ça en
plein bazar! . . . En pleine vaisselle! . . .
La pyramide de compotiers . . . assiettes!
Ah! tonnerre! . . . Une cataracte! . . . Le
vieux il étrangle de furie . . . La cliente
qu'est devant au comptoir elle glapit . . .
elle bêle d'horreur . . . Elle veut se sau-
ver! . . . elle peut pas! . . . Tout retombe
sur elle! (<u>G-B</u>, 147)

(He stumbles again . . . Bam! . . . he
lurches flops . . . headlong . . . collapses
into the shop . . . A dead weight . . . Right
into the whole mess! . . . Right into the
dishes! . . . A pyramid of fruit dishes . . .
plates! Good lord! . . . A cataract! . . .
The old fellow is speechless with rage . . .
The customer at the counter lets out a yelp .
. . she's bleating in terror . . . She wants
to get away! . . . she can't! . . . Everything falls on top of her!)

Boro, presumably drunk, has stumbled into an unexpected situation: his own fall is that of the first domino; at the end of the chain lies the customer covered with dishes.

All of these examples are comical--a Zouave crying "Vive la France" as he stumbles into a pit, a detective trampled in a bar as the customers drink to his health, a musician knocking over a pile of pawned dishes onto the pawnbroker's customer. Yet each of these humorous scenes is a translation of a serious concept. To fall and be covered by a weight is in fact one of Céline's metaphors for existence, which he elaborates explicitly and unhumorously in Voyage: "il faut retomber au bas de la muraille, chaque soir, sous l'angoisse de ce lendemain, toujours plus précaire, plus sordide" (V, 199: "every evening you fall back to the bottom of the wall beneath the anguish of the next day, ever more precarious, more sordid"). It is easy enough to fall, to be knocked down or simply borne down by the weight of anxiety. It is difficult to begin again, but to begin again is to be alive.

The humor in Guignol's Band does not disguise the fact that it is a tale of falling "beneath the anguish of the next day," that any step may lead to a fall, that to fall is not to die, but merely to be buried alive, that the weight may be removed temporarily but will not disappear.

Borokrom experiments with the sensation of falling to death when he smokes drugs and jumps down the stairs. He drags himself up the staircase step by step, turns around, and "Vlaoum! . . . Il s'envoye au vide!" (G-B, 189: "Zoom!

. . . He throws himself into empty space!"). Delighted, he
climbs up again, still smoking his pipe: "Il se relance! . .
. de plus en plus haut! . . . Il s'est arraché toute l'o-
reille! . . . Il est plein de sang à présent!" (G-B, 189:
"He hurls himself again! . . . higher and higher! . . . He's
torn off a whole ear! . . . He's covered with blood now!").

To a certain extent, Borokrom represents the artist in
Guignol's Band; as a musician he is unquestionably the most
artistic in a bizarre assortment of unsavory characters. His
fall is a distorted imitation of flying, the physical reflec-
tion of a temporary mental aberration. In attempting to soar
downward, he comes very near death. Borokrom's experiment is
similar to Bardamu's exploration of the night in that he deliberately throws himself to the bottom and learns something
about the nature of death. Bardamu's narration of his Voyage
is a journal of descent into night. Borokrom too recounts
his adventure, but his audience is more limited--Cascade and
company. Borokrom's is a story within a story; it is Ferdinand who narrates Guignol's Band.

After his fall in Normance, the doctor realizes he has
found Evil. He has always hated Jules; now he labels the
painter as the source of all problems:

> Le Mal c'est pas tout le monde qui l'a! je
> le connais moi le Mal dans sa caisse! là-
> haut, comme il est joli! . . . ivrogne, pis-
> sat, cochon, satyre! tronc! scélérat! (N,
> 27)

> (It's not everyone who has found Evil! I
> know Evil in his box! up there, isn't he

pretty! . . . drunkard, pisser, pig, old
goat! half-man! villain!)

Jules, the wicked artist, appeared on the windmill when the
doctor fell on his head. The two artists (for the doctor is
a writer) are engaged in a battle to destroy each other. Yet
he and Jules need each other, are bound together: "moi je le
mettrais sous un tas de paille comme les Hindoues nichent
leurs cobras et qu'ils peuvent plus s'en séparer" (N, 15:
"I'd put him under a pile of straw the way Hindus house their
cobras to the point where they can't do without them any
more"). The evil in Jules is the evil in the doctor, conveniently lodged in an ugly, malignant half-body, perched in
the sky calling down disaster on him, like one of his own
books which his fall has thrown into the public eye, and
which has caused him untold difficulties.

The initial fall in Normance has transformed a mundane
doctor's existence into an epic battle between his vulnerable
paranoid self and his aggressive shadow. The doctor is convinced that Jules actually called the bombers and directed
the attack:

> le Jules est revenu aux gestes! . . . il fait
> le chef d'orchestre! il oriente avec sa
> canne . . . une rafale . . . brrroum! . . .
> et encore une autre! . . . il attire toute
> une charge d'avions . . . tout un cyclone!
> (N, 40)

> (Jules is gesturing again! . . . he's like an
> orchestra conductor! he directs with his
> cane . . . one volley . . . boom! . . . and
> then another! . . . he calls a whole airplane
> charge . . . a whole cyclone!)

The doctor has fallen into a nightmare in which he (as Jules) seeks to destroy himself (as doctor).

None of these experiments with death has actually killed. Death requires an agent. Most of the murderers, both real and hypothetical, involve a person being pushed or thrown--either down the stairs, into a cesspool, or under a metro train.

Pushers

Pushing is the preferred method of murder, and many of the characters are pushed and fall to their deaths. The act of pushing is a form of wish-fulfillment: a single gesture, normally harmless, disposes of an enemy and changes the life of the pusher.

Among those murdered are old lady Henrouille (Voyage), Claben and Mille-Pattes (G-B), the Landrat and the paraplegic von Leiden (Nord). Robinson, who went blind the first time he tried to kill the old lady, regains his sight fully after he pushes her down the vault steps and she dies. While he was blind the old lady had supported him by showing the mummies to tourists; Madelon had cooked for him and promised to marry him. After killing the old lady, Robinson realizes that he does not want to marry Madelon and be taken care of for the rest of his life. As he says to Bardamu, "Un matin, pendant qu'elles étaient parties aux commissions la mère et elle, j'ai fait comme toi t'avais fait, un petit paquet, et je me suis tiré en douce . . . " (V, 447: "One morning, while she and her mother were out shopping, I did like you did, I made up a little bundle, and I slipped off . . . "). While he pretends to be following Bardamu, he is actually preceding him in the direction of death. His eyes are literally opened to the monotony of his life in Toulouse, which he rejects first for a voluntary imprisonment in the asylum where Bardamu works (to persuade Madelon he is insane), then for his own murder, which he achieves by "pushing" Madelon to kill him.

Murder introduces a new dimension to Robinson's life, as if the old lady's death had contaminated his own life and jolted him into a new existence which will be his until his own death. The push was a conscious decision; he chose to eliminate the old lady and leave Toulouse. When Madelon shoots Robinson, she is completing the action he began himself; the two murders complement each other: Robinson has chosen to die; in fact, he leaps into death: "Il est parti d'un coup comme s'il avait pris son élan" (V, 487: "He took off all at once as if he had taken a running start").

In Guignol's Band Delphine tells Claben, Boro, and Ferdinand a strange tale. After leaving Claben's house at night to look for a doctor, she returns, her hands full of cigarettes, to explain that she met a little dark man, or rather that he fell on her, and he told her to give Claben the magic leaves to smoke. "Il avait comme chuté sur elle de tout en haut du réverbère! en plein comme ça sur son chapeau . . . " (G-B, 184: "He had sort of dropped on top of her from the top of a street lamp! right onto her hat . . ."). He called himself "the Physicist from the Sky," but the cigarettes he gives her will soon lead to Claben's death rather than his recovery. The four of them smoke the drug; then Boro, imitating the mysterious heavenly provider, throws himself down the stairs, and finally he and Ferdinand throw Claben down the stairs.

They stuff Claben with his gold, then throw him on the floor to make him vomit: "O! hiss! . . . et pflof! . . . lâchez tout! . . . Pfouff!!! sur la dalle son crâne si dur!" (G-B, 199: "Heave ho! . . . and plop! . . . let go! . . . oof!!! his head so hard against the stone floor!"). Odd alchemists, they seek to transmute gold into regurgitation. To their amazement, Claben does not throw up, so they take him up the stairs and throw him down: "Vraoum! Si ça sonne! vraoum! sa grosse tête! . . . ça secoue tout l'étage du choc!" (G-B, 200: "Bam! What a noise! bam! his huge head! . . . the shock rattles the whole floor!"). Only then do they discover that Claben's head has split open. At this point the friendship between the two ends. Boro sets fire to the house and escapes to tell Cascade that Ferdinand was the murderer. Borokrom has become the evil artist that we see again in the Jules of Normance. Ferdinand is led to commit another murder by his altered perception of his surroundings. Totally paranoid, he suspects Mille-Pattes of betraying him by taking him to Cascade, so he pushes Mille-Pattes onto the tracks in the subway. Just before the train arrives, he sees Inspector Matthew on the other side of the tracks: "qui c'est qu'est là? . . . là vis à vis? . . . Ah pardon! Ah! j'écarquille! . . . Son raglan! . . . son mou! . . . sa gueule! . . . Matthew là!" (G-B, 241: "who's that over there? . . . there across the way? . . . Oh oh! my eyes are popping! . . . It's his raglan! . . . his fedora! . . . his face! . . . there's Matthew!"). It is undoubtedly the suspicious detective that he really wants to kill, but Mille-Pattes happens to be at hand, and pushing him off the platform is an easy act of defiance, although it is very likely to lead to his capture and execution.

Next Ferdinand tries to re-enlist in the French army. From the moment he sees Matthew, Ferdinand seems bent on self-destruction. After killing a man under the eyes of a police detective, he runs straight to the French embassy. He is repeating Robinson's flight from Toulouse, but he does not succeed in getting himself killed. His will to live revives when he is thrown out of the embassy and meets Sosthène. As Ferdinand tells his story to Sosthène, he regains a sense of direction--the narrative flow. Becoming a narrator gives him a new existence.

No one knows who killed the Landrat in _Nord_, and while it is assumed that von Leiden was dropped by Nicolas, who was employed to carry him, there is no apparent motive and Nicolas does not confess. Both of the bodies are found in cesspools. Their deaths constitute the denouement of the novel and the lives of almost all the inhabitants of Zornhof are changed as a consequence. The doctor and his group leave for Sigmaringen; the residents of the castle are sent into exile on a distant estate.

Both the Landrat and the fils von Leiden were hated by many, but almost everyone in town was attending a performance by a band of gypsies at the time of the crime. In any case little attempt is made to solve the mysterious murders; as we have seen with the other fatal falls, the murderer is never apprehended. The push-murders are strictly wish-fulfillment fantasies: a gesture which under ordinary circumstances would be harmless, even an expression of impotence, achieves very desirable results with a minimum of effort. From the novelist's point of view, the murders serve a similar function: he is rid of an unwanted character, the narrative pace accelerates, and the murderer becomes a fugitive--all at very little expense. Only the fall of old lady Henrouille is adequately prepared in earlier chapters; all the others are echoes of the original--unexpected, unexplained murders swiftly introduced and rapidly executed, resulting in immediate flight from the scene of the crime and intense feelings of paranoia (but not guilt) on the part of the protagonist.

One other form of assisted fall remains to be examined: the hypothetical murders. Bardamu on the <u>Amiral Braqueton</u> is detested by everyone on board, including the captain.

> Régulièrement au réveil il s'enquérait de mes nouvelles auprès des autres lurons, si «l'on» ne m'avait pas encore «balancé par-dessus bord» qu'il demandait «comme un glaviot!» Pour faire image, il crachait dans la mer mousseuse. Quelle rigolade! (<u>V</u>, 115)

> (Every morning on awakening he asked the other guys for news of me, if I hadn't yet been "tossed overboard" he would ask "like spittle!" To illustrate, he spat into the frothy sea. What a joke!)

Although the ship has met with no pronounced ill luck, everyone seems to consider Bardamu a Jonah, presumably because he is the only paying passenger, and the government employees resent his freedom. Their attitude is that to dispose of him will be a patriotic act, restore a desirable homogeneity to their group, and provide some entertainment in the meantime.

The doctor feels the same way about Jules on the windmill. He thinks that if Jules were gone, life would resume its normal course, the crazy night of bombing would end: "cet individu Jules néfaste, j'aurais voulu qu'il plonge, c'est tout! je l'aurais poussé moi, de sa plateforme!" (N, 63: "this baleful individual Jules, I would have liked to see him take a dive, that's all! I would have pushed him off his platform myself!"). Since the doctor believes that Jules is an incarnation of evil, his desire to annihilate Jules by pushing him off the windmill is an accurate and appropriate wish-fulfillment dream. In fact, Jules' power will be exorcised by a woman, Mimi, but in fantasy, the doctor saves the city by a timely murder.

The pusher disposes of another character as easily as if he had crossed his name out with a pen. As a narrative device, the murder gives the murderer authorial status. He controls the existence of another character and the direction of his own life. Within the fiction, the motivation for the murder is slight, the retribution is negligible, and the effect is to move the action into the realm of fantasy.

The transition from the labyrinth, a conscious perception of the organization of space, to the underground, a
shadow-filled other world, is made by falling. The labyrinth
is the entrance to the underground, but the descent is
abrupt, triggering the metamorphosis of a protagonist into a
narrator. When the underground is reached by a fall (remini-
scent of the birth trauma) the result is the genesis of the
work of art.

Notes

[1]Gilbert Durand, Les Structures anthropologiques de l'imaginaire (Paris: Bordas, 1969), p. 123.

[2]Durand, p. 127.

[3]Allen Thiher, Céline: The Novel as Delirium (New Brunswick, NJ: Rutgers Univ. Press, 1972), p. 157. Thiher also describes falling as a naturalistic convention and as a symbol of Céline's miserable condition. Marie-Christine Bellosta, in "Féerie pour une autre fois I et II: Un spectacle et son prologue" (Revue des Lettres Modernes, No. 543-546, 1978, 51-52), nicely shows the novel to be the délire of a man who fell on his head.

[4]Vicente Huidobro, Altazor (Santiago de Chile: Cruz del Sur, 1949), p. 19.

[5]Northrop Frye, The Secular Scripture (Cambridge, Mass.: Harvard Univ. Press, 1976), pp. 105-106.

III

THE UNDERGROUND

Beneath the conscious labyrinth of space lies another, subconscious labyrinth; in any case, it is conventional to situate this less accessible mental space below the surface, to describe it as dark, and to consider the descent into it as both difficult and dangerous. Only the exceptional person, the hero--or as hero, the artist--successfully reaches the underground, explores it, and returns with a prize. The hero who seeks below ground is a reverse Prometheus, as Erika Ostrovsky says when she calls Céline "no Prometheus who sought after the divine flame of the gods, but rather one who has striven after that of infernal regions."[1] In his criticism of modern psychiatric methods, Baryton (the asylum director in Voyage) explicitly characterizes the other side of the mind as the infernal side, as an abyss, as the cellar of the damned. He complains to Bardamu that it is unwise to push the mind too close to the edge.

Possédés, vicieux, captieux et retors, ces
favoris de la psychiatrie récente, à coups
d'analyses superconscientes nous précipitent
aux abîmes! Un matin, si vous ne réagissez
pas, Ferdinand, vous les jeunes, nous allons
passer, comprenez-moi bien, passer! A force
de nous étirer, de nous sublimer, de nous
tracasser l'entendement, de l'autre côté de
l'intelligence, du côté infernal, celui-là,
du côté dont on ne revient pas! . . . D'ail-
leurs on dirait déjà qu'ils y sont enfermés
ces supermalins, dans la cave aux damnés, à
force de se masturber la jugeote jour après
nuit! (V, 414)

(Possessed, perverse, captious, and devious,
these minions of modern psychiatry, with
their superconscious analyses, are pushing us
over the edge! One morning, if you don't re-
act, Ferdinand, you young people, we'll all
pass over, you understand, pass over! From
all this stretching, sublimating, and derang-
ing our understanding, to the far side of intelligence, the infernal side, the side of no
return! . . . Besides which you would think
they were already shut up over there, these
superclever people, in the cellar of the
damned, what with all this masturbating the
mind day after night!)

Baryton voices the familiar fears--that reason deserts one in

the subconscious, that the descent is final because it is im-

possible to return; as Racine puts it, "on ne voit point deux

fois le rivage des morts"[2] ("No one sees twice the marches

of the dead"[3]). In this case, the return may be difficult,

but the reward is great. The novel is more than a souvenir

of the journey; it is the infernal flame, valuable in its own

right.

The actual, concrete underground (natural and artificial

caves, tunnels, and holes in the ground) exercises an undeni-

able attraction on Céline's narrators; they are continually

drawn to it and seem to be looking for something in it. When
Céline describes this underground, it is clear that something
has been gained from the experience--more, I believe, than
merely the discovery of the existence of the underground, as
Ostrovsky asserts: "He simply wishes to disclose this black
labyrinth which lies, like a filthy copy of our daylight
streets, far below their surface."[4]

The underground is unquestionably black and, like conscious space, labyrinthine. Although Céline's protagonists
rarely have restful experiences underground, and although the
subterranean space is certainly not protective, sheltering,
or womb-like, the fact that the narrators return bearing a
tale shows that they have found the underground to be a
fruitful, creative space.

Because much of the action of the novels takes place
during wartime, the characters often take shelter below
ground, where they feel secure. In each of the four novels
the enclosed subterranean shelter is at one time or another
presented as an attractive, desirable, safe place to be, and
in every case it is later shown to be either unattractive,
undesirable, unsafe, or all three. The womb image is evoked
only to be proved false.

Other underground incidents describe a hellish space, or
the scene of an ordeal to be endured. In these cases escape
is a sufficient reward for the sufferer, but not always
enough to prevent him from voluntarily returning. In the underworld man's hidden side is revealed, and the wandering

anti-hero whose ambition is to see not the Truth, but only Everything, must thoroughly explore the world below the surface.

The final group of underground images are those related to the intestines. They show the subterranean world to be full of waste material and passage through it to be in only one direction--down. Just as the intestines form the transition from the inside to the outside of the body, the underground, in the journey from life to death, is the antechamber to death.

The Toothed Womb

The first portion of _Voyage_ and the entire action of
Guignol's Band, _Normance_, and _Nord_ take place during a time
of war, when the underground appears to be a space removed
from danger, a generalized bomb shelter. The doctor in _Nord_
assumes that Hitler has a subterranean stronghold similar to
the _Reichsgesundt_, safe from spies and enemy attack: "il de-
vait être encore plus profond Adolf . . ." (_Nord_, 374:
"Adolf must have been down even deeper . . ."). When the
doctor and his party are conducted below ground by Harras,
they immediately feel secure: "cette _Reichsgesundt_ sous
terre, au moins une chose, on pouvait un peu réfléchir, on
n'aurait pas pu rue Lepic . . ." (_Nord_, 375: "one good thing
about this underground _Reichsgesundt_, you were able to think
a little, which you certainly couldn't back in the rue Lepic
. . ."). Here they are fed and housed so well that he goes
on to say later, "on se sentait tout de même un peu revivre"
(_Nord_, 381: "despite all you could feel yourself coming
alive again"). They are so comfortable there that they feel
their transfer to Zornhof much as an expulsion from the Garden of Eden.

The dangers of leaving this womb-like hideout are
brought home to them the first night they spend there, when
Lili slips out for a walk with the cat and immediately sets
off the alarm system. The _Reichsgesundt_, so like an animal's

den, is the exact opposite of Zornhof, the village on the plain, where they feel constantly exposed, in woods and castle, because there is no place to hide. But even in Zornhof the underground is identified with secrecy, safety, and sustenance, for the Rittmeister has his own kitchen in the basement where food is prepared for him to eat in private. The doctor and his friends believe they have been abandoned by Harras, who has returned to Berlin and the Reichsgesundt, an underground wonderland boasting such luxuries as a Finnish bath and swimming pool. They naturally associate open spaces with being hunted and the closed space below ground with being taken care of. Later, however, they will be glad they were forced to leave Berlin, and they recognize that Harras was right to send them away. For when Harras reappears at the end of the novel, it is with the news that the Reichsgesundt (subway stop Grünwald) has been completely destroyed by bombing.

> Je comprends que Grünwald n'existe plus . . .
> ni le télégraphe . . . ni le grand bunker . .
> . ni les confrères finlandais . . . ni les
> demoiselles dactylos . . . que tout a été
> soufflé, broyé, flambé! . . . capitolade! . .
> . deux nuits! en deux nuits seulement!
> pfff! (Nord, 686)

> (I understand that Grünwald doesn't exist any
> more . . . no more telegraph . . . no big
> bunker . . . no Finnish colleagues . . . no
> lady typists . . . the whole thing snuffed
> out, squashed, burnt up! . . . wiped out! . .
> . in two nights! just two nights! poof!)

Although existence at Zornhof is at best precarious, none of the halts on their journey has proved hospitable, and the Reichsgesundt was not a paradise but a temporary place of rest. As they look back on it, they seem to feel, as if they were Adam and Eve looking back to see the Garden in flames, that they have escaped just in time.

The mummy crypt in Toulouse appears at first to the characters of Voyage to offer the same sort of relief from persecution. Both Robinson and old lady Henrouille lived in constant fear of imprisonment before moving to Toulouse, where the crypt is to give them financial security and Robinson finds a future wife who is an admirable cook. Bardamu himself takes advantage of his first visit to the vault to kiss Robinson's fiancée. "La lanterne s'éteignait. On l'a rallumée dix fois pendant que nous arrangions le passé avec l'avenir. Elle me défendait ses seins qu'elle avait bien trop sensibles" (V, 381: "The lantern went out. We relighted it a dozen times while we arranged the past with the future. She forbade me her breasts which were far too sensitive"). The fire of passion, taking the place of the lantern, finds its place in this dark, bare hole in the ground. Bardamu feels safe from observation in the vault; it is the ideal place to seduce Madelon.

The entire episode is marked by the lighthearted behavior of the characters in the presence of death, in a sacred space next to a church, a vault constructed for and consecrated to death in its visible, concrete form: mummified bodies preserved in quicklime. The ritual question "N'est-ce pas qu'ils n'ont pas l'air tristes?" (V, 381: "They don't look unhappy now do they?") illustrates the characters' refusal to adopt a serious attitude. Each of them is looking for the easiest way to turn the vault to profit.

> La mère Henrouille avait songé à augmenter ses prix, dès son arrivée, c'était question d'entente avec l'Evêché. Seulement ça n'allait pas tout seul à cause du curé de Sainte-Eponime qui voulait prélever un tiers de la recette, rien que pour lui, et puis aussi de Robinson qui protestait continuellement parce qu'elle ne lui donnait pas assez de ristourne, qu'il trouvait. (V, 382)

> (Old lady Henrouille had been thinking of raising her prices from the moment she arrived, it was a matter to be worked out with the Diocese. Only it wasn't so easy because of the Sainte-Eponime priest who wanted to skim off a third of the profits just for himself, and then there was Robinson who was always protesting because she wasn't giving him enough of the proceeds, it seemed to him.)

The crypt is seen as an inexhaustible source of income for everyone who comes in contact with it. It is generally discussed in commercial terms, and the tone of the old lady's spiel, when she conducts visits, is scarcely one of hushed respect for the dead.

> «Notre collection est unique au monde . . . La chair a évidemment disparu . . . Seule la peau leur est restée après, mais elle est tannée. [...] Et ce grand-là avec sa chemise et de la dentelle qui est encore après . . . Il a toutes ses dents. . . Vous remarquerez . . .» Elle leur tapait sur la poitrine encore à tous pour finir et ça faisait tambour. [...] «Vous pouvez les toucher avant de vous en aller . . . Vous rendre compte par vous-

mêmes . . . Mais ne tirez pas fort dessus . .
. Je vous les recommande . . . Ils sont tout
ce qu'il y a de fragile . . .» (V, 382)

("Our collection is unique in the world . . .
Naturally the flesh has disappeared . . . Only the skin is left on them, but it's tanned.
[...] And that tall one over there with his
shirt and some lace still hanging on it . . .
He has all his teeth . . . You'll notice . .
." She thumped them all on the chest at the
end and it sounded like a drum. [...] "You
can touch them before leaving . . . To get an
idea . . . But don't pull too hard . . .
Please be careful . . . They're fragile as
can be . . .")

Using the very words of a horse-trader ("He has all his
teeth"), of a cheese-seller ("you can touch them") of an an-
tique dealer ("They're fragile as can be"), she turns the
visit into a circus sideshow accompanied by drumming on the
hollow chests. The effect is somewhat ghoulish, as if Madelon's delicious meals were prepared from the vanished flesh
of the mummies. It is certainly a change for Bardamu, who
has become so involved in his practice that he feels responsible for all the deaths in his neighborhood. He felt particularly guilty about the death of the child Bébert, whom he
had tried so hard to save. Yet he knows that his livelihood
also depends on death. This vacation in Toulouse is, like
the war episode, an interlude among people who have no genuine concept of death. Throughout the novel he makes this
startling discovery over and over again, that others cannot
imagine death. He attributes Madelon's indifference to death
to the times in which she was brought up and her lack of experience.

> La mort ne lui disait rien à elle cette mi-
> gnonne. Elle était née pendant la guerre,
> temps de la mort légère. Moi, je savais bien
> comment on meurt. J'ai appris. Ça fait
> souffrir énormément. (V, 381)

> (Death didn't mean a thing to this little
> cutie. She was born during the war, when
> death was cheap. I myself knew just what
> death meant. I've learned. It causes terri-
> ble suffering.)

Those who cannot imagine death live as if they were not to die: this to Céline is monstrous. "Le colonel, c'était donc un monstre! A présent, j'en étais assuré, pire qu'un chien, il n'imaginait pas son trépas!" (V, 17: "The colonel was a monster! Now I was sure of it, he was worse than a dog, he couldn't conceive of his own death!")

There is a certain justice to the sudden end to every-one's exploitation of the crypt, which has the cheerful air of a love grotto (pay on the way out). Death reasserts its sinister self when the old lady falls down the stairs and dies, as if her schemes were being foiled not by Robinson, but by the crypt itself. The crypt is death, to be trifled with, quarreled over, exploited in every way, but not to be avoided in the end. Bardamu's precipitate departure from Toulouse is more than a fear of being implicated in a murder: it is a flight from death as he has seen it, the only exit from the underground. Life begins in a womb, and it is le-gitimate to seek protection and renewal of life in a cave, the earth's womb; we find instead the jaws of death driving people forth.

Eliade, in his discussion of the subterranean womb,[5] speaks of "the earth depicted as a giant Mother," the cavern as a place of initiation and rebirth. In prehistoric times funerals were held in caves in order to return the dead to their mother to be reborn. Such faith in a post-mortem rena- scence is entirely lacking in Céline. All his writings posit death as an end-point to existence of any kind, with little joy to be found along the way.

The mythological prototype for the image of the under- ground as an inviting womb with death lurking inside is Poly- phemus' cave. Odysseus and his men are immediately struck by the civilized aspect of the cave:

> But when we had arrived at the place, which was nearby, there at the edge of the land we saw the cave, close to the water, high, and overgrown with laurels, and in it were sta- bled great flocks, sheep and goats alike, and there was a fenced yard built around it with a high wall of grubbed-out boulders and tall pines and oaks with lofty foliage.[6]

They enter, admire everything inside, help themselves to the cheeses, and wait for the owner to come home. As G. S. Kirk has pointed out, Polyphemus' behavior is all the more sur- prising because he is at first presented as a conscientious herdsman who seems to eat no meat. He is fond of his flocks and tends them with devotion. His change of behavior when confronted by Odysseus is dramatic and unexpected. Unmoved by Odysseus' plea for hospitality and invocation of Zeus, Polyphemus grabs two of the companions, dashes them to the ground, and devours them whole, like a wild animal. He polishes off his feast with unwatered wine, "always for the Greeks a sign of boorishness, imprudence or greed."[7]

The transformation of Polyphemus from a peaceful goatherd to a devouring monster and of his cave from a refuge to a slaughterhouse illustrates the impossible nature of man's dream to return to the womb in which he was created. A mother will push away her young if they try to nurse when they are too big. They cannot return to the womb--they don't fit. The vagina dentata is an enduring image for the harshness of life, where the remembered world of the womb can never be re-entered. Impossible as the dream is, it decks the cave with the appearance of security, an appearance which cannot be trusted.

An underground womb well-equipped with teeth is the basement of Claben's house in Guignol's Band. Ferdinand and Borokrom, with a dead body on their hands, decide to take it down to the cellar, the closest thing to a tomb in the house. The underground is undeniably attractive--"dans la cave c'était déjà mieux" (G-B, 213: "in the cellar it was somewhat better"), says Ferdinand--but when Boro closes the trap door on him and throws a bomb, what had seemed an ideal hiding place bursts into flames, and the smoke drives him from a hole in which he had expected to find shelter. Again the underground is not the refuge it appears. Céline's protagonists repeatedly retreat to underground shelters which eject them forcibly. The womb-like appearance of the underground is deceptive; we are always reminded that there is no shelter in this world, and those who escape the underground will encounter death elsewhere.

Hellbound

When a search party in <u>Nord</u> comes upon a hitherto unsus-
pected hole in the plain where a number of women are hiding,
the scene is far more hellish than womb-like. Not only are
the women savagely attacking two men in their midst, they are
cooking, in a witch-like rite, a captured horse:

> C'est une crevasse . . . ils sont combien au
> fond là-dedans? . . . pas ils! elles! . . .
> tous des femmes! . . . autour d'un feu de
> bois . . . elles ont dû amener du bois de
> loin! . . . pas un petit feu, un vrai bûcher!
> . . . elles ont mis quelque chose à cuire,
> sur le feu, à même . . . pas étonnant qu'on
> voyait rien de loin, cette crevasse est très
> profonde, avec une petite mare au bout . . .
> elles se sont établi un campement . . . elles
> se font la cuisine . . . plutôt elles se font
> brûler des viandes . . . que ça sent si fort!
> (<u>Nord</u>, 609-610)

> (It's a gully . . . how many men are down
> there? . . . not men! women! . . . all of
> them women! . . . around a wood fire . . .
> they must have brought the wood a long way! .
> . . not a little fire, a real bonfire! . . .
> they've put something on to cook, right on
> the fire . . . not surprising we didn't see
> anything from a distance, the gully is very
> deep, with a little pool of water at the end
> . . . they've made camp . . . they're cooking
> . . . or rather they're burning some meat . .
> . what a stench!)

Here we have a grotesque caricature of the <u>Reichsgesundt</u>,
with a filthy pond full of horse entrails in place of the
Finnish bath, screaming prostitutes instead of smiling secre-
taries. The doctor's role is reversed: he is not required
to leave the hole; he invades it to save the count and the

Revizor, who are being beaten by the women. The predominance of females makes the hole, as a non-womb, all the more perverted. It is also a distorted transposition of the count's basement kitchens. The count himself is not able to join the villagers as they feast on the singed horsemeat left by the fleeing women. Formerly a hoarder, he is forced to watch his rescuers eating the remains of his own mare. The scene is one of near-cannibalism, with the horse substituted for the count, the "Rittmeister," who later dies from his brutal treatment. It recalls a similar scene of butchery in Voyage, where Bardamu is overcome by a fit of vomiting as beef and mutton are distributed to the soldiers in the heat of a summer's day.

> C'était donc dans une prairie d'août qu'on distribuait toute la viande pour le régiment, --ombrée de cerisiers et brûlée déjà par la fin de l'été. Sur des sacs et des toiles de tentes largement étendues et sur l'herbe même, il y en avait pour des kilos et des kilos de tripes étalées, de gras en flocons jaunes et pâles, des moutons éventrés avec leurs organes en pagaïe, suintant en ruisselets ingénieux dans la verdure d'alentour, un boeuf entier sectionné en deux, pendu à l'arbre, et sur lequel s'escrimaient encore en jurant les quatre bouchers du régiment pour lui tirer des morceaux d'abattis. (V, 24)

> (So it was in an August meadow that all the meat for the regiment was distributed--shaded with cherry trees and already burned by the end of the summer. On sacks and stretched out tent canvas, and right on the grass, there were kilos and kilos of tripe spread out, yellow and pale flakes of fat, disemboweled sheep with their organs all over the place, oozing ingenious rivulets into the surrounding verdure, an entire steer cut in half, hung from a tree, over which the four

butchers of the regiment were fencing and
swearing, extracting the giblets.)

The implicit comparison between the slaughter of war and the
cutting up of a beef carcass is thoroughly nauseating. The
fencing butchers attack the meat exactly as they would an enemy. That this enemy will end up in someone's stomach is
scarcely an appetizing thought. Bardamu is not a vegetarian;
it is not meat-eating, but war, that he condemns. By trans-
posing the war to an extraction of giblets in a meadow, he
both belittles its noble cause and reveals it for the figurative cannibalism it is.

In Nord, the distribution of meat is accompanied by a
parody of civilized manners, as if the action were set in an
expensive restaurant.

> un romani qui découpe . . . petites tranches?
> minces? . . . ou des épaisses . . . il nous
> demande notre goût? . . . on voit qu'il est à
> son affaire . . . en temps de paix il doit
> servir, il a du style . . . il doit être
> quelque chose dans un hôtel ou restaurant . .
> . ce qu'on préfère? . . . dans le gigot? . .
> . l'encolure? . . . il faudra en remporter,
> on pourra jamais tout finir . . . ça sera en-
> core bon . . . (Nord, 614)

> (a gypsy does the carving . . . small slices?
> thin? . . . or thick? . . . he's asking our
> preference? . . . you can tell he's in his
> element . . . in peacetime he must be a wait-
> er, he has style . . . he must do something
> in a hotel or restaurant . . . what's our
> pleasure? . . . the leg? . . . the neck? . .
> . we'll have to take some home, we'll never
> be able to finish it . . . it will still be
> good . . .)

The Reichsgesundt and the basement kitchens were orderly uses
of the underground with civilized overtones of greed and
elitism; the fire-filled hole on the plain reveals another,
ugly side of human nature--that people can devour raw meat
and beat others to death. The doctor's descent into this
simulacrum of hell has given him a glimpse beneath the surface. Above ground people eat watery soup, below ground they
eat each other.

Bardamu makes a similar discovery about Americans in New
York when he notices a policeman watching him and needs a
place to hide. To escape the street he goes into the nearby
entrance to the underground toilets. The passage which follows on what he calls "le communisme joyeux du caca" ("the
joyful communism of shitting") cannot be considered a favora-
ble description of American toilet habits. The place is like
a swimming pool emptied of its water, filled with a dying
light and crimson unbuttoned men pushing their dirty business
in public, making odd noises. He is particularly struck by
the difference between Americans above and below ground,
well-groomed and serious in the street, noisy and sloppy in
the bathroom. Obviously the actual activities are no different from those in French toilets. What seems to shock Bardamu, apart from the lack of privacy, is the change from daylight to the "jour mourant" ("dying light"), from the surface
to the underground, to a place of dying.

>Ce contraste était bien fait pour déconcerter
>un étranger. Tout ce débraillage intime,

> cette formidable familiarité intestinale et
> dans la rue cette parfaite contrainte! (V,
> 196)

> (This contrast was just the thing to discon-
> cert a foreigner. All this intimate unbut-
> toning, this remarkable intestinal familiar-
> ity, and in the street such perfect con-
> straint!)

He calls the place "the fecal cavern," and he finds the odor
so offensive he soon leaves. This underground space is consecrated to excrement, just as the mummy crypt is consecrated
to death. There is a dress code and a ritual exchange of di-
alogue. The subterranean side of people is as highly organized as their formal street behavior; the underground temple
is the seat of the cult of the under side. It is the hidden
side of people, the side they are ashamed to show by daylight, that Bardamu seeks to know by journeying through the
underground.

In Normance the underground is given more animate form
in the hole which suddenly appears in the hall, a hole which
opens and closes like the jaws of a monster, presenting a
further obstacle to the building's occupants, already blinded
by bombs, shaken by explosives, parched by thirst, and
threatened by the animosity of their fellows. For a time everyone scampers around the sides of the hole; repeated attempts to cross it on one errand or another meet with failure, an exercise in futility. Eventually the hole vanishes
as abruptly as it appeared. It was only one scene in a giant
Bosch-like painting of hell:

ce que j'aperçois comme crevasse! . . . en
plein milieu du couloir . . . trois fois
large comme tout à l'heure . . . et qui min-
cit . . . rapetisse . . . referme et reouvre!
. . . toute la longueur du couloir! jusqu'à
la rue . . . jusqu'aux pavés . . . un gouffre
mouvant dans le couloir! je vous mens pas .
. . un gouffre! (N, 179-180)

(what a pit I see! . . . right in the middle
of the hall . . . three times as wide as before . . . and getting narrower . . . smaller
. . . reclosing and reopening! . . . the
whole length of the hall! out to the street
. . . all the way to the pavement . . . a
moving chasm in the hall! I'm not exaggerating . . . a chasm!)

Such a monster, big-bellied and mouth agape, must remind
us of the mythological guardians at the threshold of the land
of the dead. Before reaching the underworld, the hero must
pass its demons. "They are preliminary embodiments of the
dangerous aspect of the presence, corresponding to the mythological ogres that bound the conventional world, or to the
two rows of teeth of the whale."[8] The whale itself, or the
actual underground, from which the hero should emerge purified and reborn, lies beyond the hall-hole, in the elevator
shaft.

The elevator is the vertical link "from cellar to attic," the concrete representation of the vertical orientation
of a dwelling Bachelard speaks of in his study of literary
space. The house is polarized by the opposition of the ra-
tional attic to the irrational cellar. Bachelard does not
see such verticality in an apartment building ("Elevators destroy the heroisms of the staircase"), but rather a stack of

horizontal living spaces.[9] This apartment building, however, is the scene of considerable vertical movement in the stair-well and an intermingling of tenants which denies privacy to anyone in any part of the building. The elevator assumes an important role on the first page of the novel, when the nar-rator falls down it. Later we discover the shaft has an un-usual characteristic--it sucks people in. The doctor tells us that he and his companions have a choice: to be catapult-ed to the stars by the explosions, or "être pompés au cou-loir, aspirés au trou d'ascenseur, syphonnés!" (N, 114: "be pumped in the hall, sucked into the elevator hole, siphoned off!"). The elevator car conveniently out of the way, or stopped at whichever floor the narrator thinks appropriate (he changes his mind from one line to the next), the open shaft acts as a siphon, and a group of people who have been sucked into it collects at the bottom. The elevator should facilitate communication between floors and ease the transi-tion from, for example, the upper and lower classes, if the building is taken to represent society, the conscious and the subconscious if the building is the mind. But this elevator shaft has a malevolent mind of its own, and it does not carry people up, only down: "c'est fait! si vite fait! rien sen-ti! enfournés! tous sous l'ascenseur! on se retrouve tous! cinquante là-dessous!" (N, 196: "it's done! done so fast! didn't feel a thing! gobbled up! all under the elevator! we're all together again! fifty under there!"). The choice of the word "enfournés," which can mean either "put in the oven" or "put in one's mouth," reinforces the image of the hole as a giant beast.

Another figurative sojourn in hell--does this mean another exposition of the insight gained into the hidden side of man? In this case, the narrator returns with a blazing vision set forth in 375 pages, the novel itself. The doctor fell on his head and described what he saw afterward. As one grotesque incident succeeds another in the novel, it becomes obvious that it is not at all the faithful chronicle the doctor had promised; he even concedes:

> Ah, que vous écriez, salaud! il hallucine, l'hargneux cocu! . . . rien du tout tel est arrivé! . . . il invente! brodouille! délate! venime! daube! y avait d'autres un peu qu'étaient là! qu'ont rien vu! ni de moulin! ni de Jules! ni de Déluge! (N, 142)

> (Ah, you're shouting, the son of a bitch! he's hallucinating, the cantankerous old fart! . . . nothing of the sort happened! . . . he's making it up! adding on! denouncing! poisoning! jeering! there were a few others around at the time! who didn't see a thing! no windmill! no Jules! no Flood!)

Normance is the tale of one who has descended into the underground and seen what men try to hide. The novel is full of subterranean images, as the doctor himself points out: "je vous parle que de crevasses, je m'aperçois . . . celle du ciel! . . . celle du couloir! . . . celle sous l'ascenseur!" (N, 213: "all I'm talking about is chasms, I can see . . . the one in the sky! . . . the one in the hall! . . . the one under the elevator!"). Each of these forms of the underground contributes to a picture of a voluntary visitor to hell, the man who is determined to explore unknown nether regions, the black side of the soul, and return to tell the tale.

The explosive cellar in _Guignol's Band_ and the bombardment in _Normance_ are both fiery undergrounds, and the destruction they wreak is almost fatal to the explorer. His narrow escape from death endows him with a prestige which sets him apart from other men and lends weight to his story. He has been struck by lightning; he has power.

Tripe

Bardamu's first encounter with the underground in Voyage takes place in Paris while he is recuperating from his war wound and living with Musyne. During an air alert, when Musyne wants to take shelter with the neighbors, Bardamu minimizes the danger:

> Ces paniques menues pendant lesquelles tout un quartier en pyjama, derrière la bougie, disparaissait en gloussant dans les profondeurs pour échapper à un péril presque entièrement imaginaire, mesuraient l'angoissante futilité de ces êtres tantôt poules effrayées, tantôt moutons fats et consentants. (V, 82)

> (These petty panics during which an entire neighborhood in pajamas, behind a candle, disappeared clucking into the depths to escape a peril almost purely imaginary were a measure of the heartbreaking futility of these beings by turns scared chickens or silly and accepting sheep.)

Nevertheless he might have followed the terrified Musyne, had it not been the butcher's cellar the neighbors chose as their shelter. Across the threshold wafted an acrid and familiar odor that Bardamu could not tolerate. This well-known odor, the same one that had nauseated Bardamu when the soldiers divided up animal carcasses at the front, is identified with the carnage of war. He refuses to enter the cellar, refuses butchery, and loses his girl friend. Thus he has transformed his refusal of war into a heroic act, while the sheep-like crowds flocking to the underground shelters and condoning slaughter are "scared chickens" and "silly and accepting sheep." Bardamu the coward is the only one to recognize and condemn the blind fear and conformism which create war.

In this early episode we discover the elements which are consistently associated with the underground: it is attractive, promising a factitious shelter; it is full, usually of hostile people; it contains food or the prospect of financial gain (in this case both); the narrator rejects it, often because of its odor. All of the images already discussed convey one or more of these qualities. The combination, when we take up the group of images related to the Underground, or metro, forms a pattern which is distinctly intestinal.

After escaping from Claben's basement in Guignol's Band, Ferdinand encounters Mille-Pattes, and in order to get rid of him, he pushes him in front of an Underground train. There is little or no motivation for this murder, although the implication is that Ferdinand suspects Mille-Pattes of duplicity, or that, universally blamed for Claben's death, for which he was only partially responsible, he compensates by killing Mille-Pattes outright.

> Ferdinand! Ferdinand! je me dis . . . T'es
> la victime d'un complot! . . . y a pas d'er-
> reur on te veut du mal! . . . mal à la tête!
> . . . c'est la preuve! Es-tu régulier? . . .
> C'est la question qui me bouleverse . . .
> Claben t'avait-il fait du tort? . . . Tu l'as
> volé donc que pour boire? Personne n'a la
> preuve! . . . Mille-Pattes non plus! . . . Il
> est sous le métro à présent! . . . Il est en-
> core plus petit! . . . Ça y apprendra à faire
> l'arsouille! (G-B, 289)

("Ferdinand! Ferdinand!" I said to myself .
. . "You're the victim of a conspiracy! . . .
make no mistake they mean you harm! . . .
they'll have your head! . . . the evidence is
there! Are you an decent guy? . . . That's
the burning question . . . Had Claben ever
done you wrong? . . . Did you steal from him
just for drink? Nobody can prove it! . . .
Not even Mille-Pattes! . . . He's under the
metro train now! . . . That'll teach him to
double-cross!")

Again he has gone below ground to dispose of a body, this
time to the subway, that maze of tunnels which, as J.-P.
Richard has pointed out, demands an intestinal interpretation: "Le métro, [...] figure, peu déguisée, du long défilé
intestinal"[10] ("The metro, [...] image, scarcely disguised,
for the long march of the intestines"). For Ferdinand the
underground has become a symbolic garbage dump, a convenient
place to dispose of the refuse he accumulates in his wander-
ings.

Céline himself has mentioned the importance of the subway to his work, in Entretiens avec le Professeur Y, where he
describes his writing style as an "emotional metro." Normance in particular contains repeated references to the metro. It is an almost legendary place, often mentioned but
never visited by the protagonists. In fact, Normance opens
with the narrator's expressed intention of taking shelter in
the metro, which, however, he never reaches: "on allait au
métro, c'est tout!" (N, 375: "we were just on our way to
the metro, that's all!").

The metro station where one embarks on a tortuous underground journey may easily be recognized as the point of departure for the adventure that Bardamu in <u>Voyage</u> likened to
the journey of life. Yet the metro is the very place the
doctor never goes. This is partly explained by his convic-
tion that the crowds of people in the metro will be hostile
to him (as indeed they are in <u>Nord</u>):

> mais elles sont dans le métro, les foules! .
> . . les maisons vont s'écrouler, elles font
> bien de se tapir les foules! de se terrer
> sous les égouts! j'irais aussi moi-même de
> même, si j'avais pas ce que vous savez, cette
> réputation germaneuse, «collaborante», mor-
> telle! . . . ils me lyncheraient peut-être au
> métro s'ils décelaient ma présence! (<u>N</u>, 23)

> (but they're in the metro, the crowds! . . .
> the houses are going to collapse, they're
> right to take cover, the crowds! to go to
> ground under the sewers! I'd go myself if I
> didn't have what you already know about, that
> reputation for Germanizing, "collaborating,"
> fatal! . . . they might lynch me in the metro
> if they detected my presence!)

The doctor expects to be persecuted as a scapegoat. Bardamu's experience on the <u>Amiral Braqueton</u> is projected on the
hypothetical crowds in the metro. Instead, the very treatment that he anticipated in the metro is liberally dealt out
to him by his neighbors in the apartment building during the
rest of the novel.

Nevertheless the feces are highly prized by their maker
and hold monetary significance for him. This is why the underground so often contains something precious, usually edi-
ble. In <u>Normance</u> the cellars are rumored to be vast stock-

piles of food and drink. Throughout the narrative the words
"à la cave!" ("to the cellars!") excite feverish but ulti-
mately fruitless activity on the part of the tenants. They
have visions of hidden treasure buried in some secret inac-
cessible chamber. The meat in the butcher's cellar of Voyage
is, like the feces, both valuable and repulsive. Rejection
of the cellars is both self-denial and modesty. By frequently mentioning the sewers together with the metro in Normance
(as in the passage cited above), the narrator establishes a
tacit comparison which reflects unfavorably on those taking
shelter in the metro. The doctor, in holding himself aloof
from the flight to the metro, is rejecting the double association fear/intestines, which his neighbors nevertheless act
out for him under the table by mingling their excrement in a
common puddle.

In the Berlin subway, on the way to the Reichsgesundt,
the doctor and his party are mistaken for Canadian parachut-
ists; surrounded by howling urchins, they barely escape with
their lives. A passing Frenchman who comes to their rescue
is very nearly assassinated: "je voyais le moment qu'ils al-
laient le balancer sous le dur! . . . notre Picpus! . . .
seul contre mille!" (Nord, 366: "I could see it coming,
they were going to chuck him under the train! . . . our Picpus! . . . one against a thousand!"). The recurring motif
"chucking people under metro trains" adds a sinister note to
Céline's "emotional metro"--actually quite an appropriate
metaphor for a highly-charged style that will run over some

readers. The metro, like the intestinal tract, engulfs matter and carries it down, from inside the social body to outside, from life to death. Mille-Pattes dies in the Underground; Picpus almost dies in the Berlin subway. The prospective lynching in the metro of <u>Normance</u> is the imaginative equivalent of Mille-Pattes' death, an expression of the certainty that death lies at the end of the tunnel.

The intestines are the last stage of the digestive process, a process in many ways similar to the work of the writer, who "digests" his experience and presents the public with the amalgam which results. Richard remarks that for Céline writing may be equated with defecating.[11] This suggests to us that Céline is like a small child playing with his stool. The reader, who consumes the written work, may feel somewhat uneasy about his implied status as coprophagist.

The underground may be perceived as a womb, but the deception will be (literally) exploded. It may seem to be hell, but whereas Dante found through the inferno the road to salvation, for Céline it is the first stage on the way to the annihilation of being.

Above all, the underground is an intestinal image. It is a vehicle for waste disposal, especially dead bodies. It contains something precious--food or the means to earn money. It appears attractive, but is resolutely rejected by the narrator, while his neighbors take childish delight in it. It is a place of transition from above to below, and a descent into it leads to death.

But the hero who returns from the underground has found it fertile, and the prize he carries back with him is a great one. The writer who explores the underground finds that it is not after all completely dark. There are bright spots-- not glimmers, or dim glows, but intense raging fires.

Notes

[1]Erika Ostrovsky, _Céline and His Vision_ (New York: NYU Press, 1967), p. 37.

[2]_Phèdre_, Act II, Scene V.

[3]Samuel Solomon, _Jean Racine. Complete Plays_, Vol. II (New York: Random House, 1967), p. 263.

[4]Ostrovsky, p. 66.

[5]Mircea Eliade, _Myths, Dreams and Mysteries_, trans. Philip Mairet (New York: Harper and Brothers, 1960), pp. 169-172.

[6]Richmond Lattimore, trans., _The Odyssey of Homer_ (New York: Harper and Row, 1965), p. 142.

[7]G. S. Kirk, _Myth: Its Meaning and Functions in Ancient and Other Cultures_ (Berkeley: Univ. of Cal. Press, 1970), pp. 166-167.

[8]Joseph Campbell, _The Hero With a Thousand Faces_, 2nd. ed. (1949; rpt. Princeton: Princeton Univ. Press, 1973), p. 92.

[9]Gaston Bachelard, _La Poétique de l'espace_ (Paris: PUF, 1958), p. 42.

[10]Jean-Pierre Richard, _Nausée de Céline_ (Paris: Fata Morgana, 1973), p. 92.

[11]Richard, p. 71.

IV

THE FIRE IN THE NIGHT

Early in Voyage au bout de la nuit, shortly after Bardamu discovers the horrors of war and the loneliness of night,
he finds consolation in watching villages burn. The weather
is dry, and every night some burning village can be found to
brighten the darkness and provide some distraction from the
constant fear Bardamu and his men feel riding about looking
for their regiment. There is a hint of pagan ritual, of St.
John's Eve festive bonfires, in these gaily burning villages
lighting up the summer's night.

> Un village brûlait toujours du côté du canon.
> On en approchait pas beaucoup, pas de trop,
> on le regardait seulement d'assez loin le
> village, en spectateurs pourrait-on dire
> [...] Ça se remarque bien comment que ça
> brûle un village, même à vingt kilomètres.
> C'était gai. Un petit hameau de rien du tout
> qu'on apercevait même pas pendant la journée,
> au fond d'une moche petite campagne, eh bien,
> on a pas idée la nuit, quand il brûle, de
> l'effet qu'il peut faire! [...] quand on a
> des feux à regarder la nuit passe bien mieux,
> c'est plus rien à endurer, c'est plus de la
> solitude. (V, 31-32)

(There was always a village burning in the
direction of the firing line. We wouldn't
get close to it, not terribly, we just
watched the village from a distance, as spec-
tators, so to speak. [...] It's very notice-
able, a village burning, even twenty kilome-
ters away. It was cheerful. A nothing little hamlet that you didn't even catch sight
of during the day, buried in an unattractive
little countryside, well, you have no idea
the impression it can make when it burns at
night! [...] when you have fires to look at
the night seems to pass more easily, it's not
something to endure any more, you don't feel
so all alone.)

There seem to be no people in these villages, no sense of

disaster, just flames to light up the night. The men watch

churches, barns, and haystacks burning and collapsing as if

they were watching a movie; they fall asleep in the fields

with a sense of security unique in the war episodes. The

fire makes the night bearable.

Fires, both large and small, from candles to full-scale

flaming bombardments, reappear frequently in Céline's novels,

generally at night. They are not always reassuring, but they

always provide light and a better look at the night. All

through Voyage Céline compares life to a night-journey; fire

is a positive element in this journey. Furthermore, accord-

ing to Gilbert Durand, "le feu est très souvent assimilé à la

parole"[1] ("fire is often equated with the word"). The writ-

ten word, or the novel, is the fire in Céline's night, and an

analysis of fire imagery shows us the role of verbal art in

Céline's imaginative space. With this in mind, a review of

his fictional fires will show them to be related to his ideas on creativity, art, and the role of the artist.

Fire consumes garbage. This is not one of the more widely recognized functions of the work of art, but the action of fire is very similar to the act of digestion, mentioned in the previous chapter. Digestion is generally believed to remove the useful parts of food and eliminate the remainder as waste; anything left over is presumably garbage. On the other hand, everyone knows that "fire purifies;" what is unconsumed must therefore be "pure." If the act of writing is seen to be related to fire, the experience is presumably cleansing. If the work itself is like fire, it is apt to burn.

Fire often becomes liquid in Céline's novels and flows like lava. There are also many explosive, eruptive scenes. The volcano is an important image. It is the Deluge returned, this time in fire. However, this deluge of fire is not divine retribution, for it is often man-made. It is the human race's attempt at self-destruction.

The third aspect of fire I will examine is its power to attract and kill like a lantern drawing moths at night. People are drawn by the flickering light on a movie screen because it makes the night a little brighter, life a little easier. The work of art is in fact a suicide on the part of the artist, for to fix anything is to kill it, and to fix one's dreams is to kill oneself.

In Africa, Bardamu falls ill and decides to leave his post in the jungle. Before leaving he takes a lesson from his experience at war and sets fire to his hut to light up the night. "Cela se passait après le coucher du soleil. Les flammes s'élevèrent rapides, fougueuses" (V, 175: "This took place after sunset. The flames rose rapidly, impetuously"). Just as fire is a form of speech and represents the written word, the fire-maker is the writer, or artist. Jules and Borokrom are outstanding examples: Jules calls down a bombardment and Borokrom throws bombs. Through the images of fire we see the artist's view of himself; he is an incendiary, a pathfinder, a Cassandra crying on the ramparts, a prophet, a sorcerer unconsumed by his own flames.

The fire-maker sees himself at least as a prophet, if not a god. He denounces the evil he sees around him and reveals what is to come. It is a thankless task, for his news is not good.

The incendiary and the arsonist are intent on destroying by fire. The writer who sees himself in such terms--as the kindler of a destructive fire--writes to destroy something, illusion perhaps, as well as literary convention. The wandering writer, the pícaro, will see much in society about which his audience must be disabused.

Dirty Linen

Fire cleanses, as Bardamu is the first to point out:

> Ma mère n'avait pas que des dictons pour
> l'honnêteté, elle disait aussi, je m'en sou-
> vins à point, quand elle brûlait chez nous
> les vieux pansements: «Le feu purifie tout!»
> (V, 175)

> (My mother had more than just sayings about
> honesty, she also used to say, as I remem-
> bered when the time came, whenever she burned
> our old bandages: "Fire purifies every-
> thing!")

It is at once apparent that Bardamu's mother is not purifying
anything whatsoever, unless it be a world full of soiled bandages, in which case she has a long way to go. She is in
fact destroying, and might more aptly have said, "Fire rids
us of unwanted garbage." Bardamu quotes her presumably to
justify his odd behavior in the jungle when, in the middle of
a drenching nocturnal rain, he sets fire to his hut and marches off into the forest with a raging fever.

> Le moment vint. Mes silex n'étaient pas très
> bien choisis, mal pointus, les étincelles me
> restaient surtout dans les mains. Enfin,
> tout de même, les premières marchandises
> prirent feu en dépit de l'humidité. C'était
> un stock de chaussettes absolument trempées.
> Cela se passait après le coucher du soleil.
> Les flammes s'élevèrent rapides, fougueuses.
> [...] Le caoutchouc nature qu'avait acheté
> Robinson grésillait au centre et son odeur me
> rappelait invinciblement l'incendie célèbre
> de la Société des Téléphones, quai de Gre-
> nelle, qu'on avait été regarder avec mon on-
> cle Charles, qui chantait lui si bien la ro-
> mance. L'année d'avant l'Exposition ça se

passait, la Grande, quand j'étais encore bien
petit. Rien ne force les souvenirs à se mon-
trer comme les odeurs et les flammes. Ma
case elle, sentait tout pareil. Bien que dé-
trempée, elle a brûlé entièrement, très fran-
chement et marchandises et tout. Les comptes
étaient faits. (V, 175)

(The time had come. My flints were poorly
chosen and badly sharpened; most of the
sparks stayed in my hands. At last, after
all, the first goods caught fire in spite of
the damp. It was a supply of socks that was
completely soaked. This took place after
sunset. The flames rose rapidly, impetuously. [...] The crude rubber Robinson had
bought sizzled in the center and its odor
brought inescapably to mind the famous fire
at the Telephone Company, on the Quai de Gre-
nelle, that I had gone to watch with my Uncle
Charles, the one who sang ballads so well.
The year before the Fair that was, the big
one, when I was still little. Nothing brings
out memories like odors and flames. My cabin
smelled just the same. Soaked as it was, it
burned to the ground, quite thoroughly, goods
and all. The score was settled.)

This passage contains repeated references to the past--to the
narrator's childhood, to his predecessor Robinson, to his
fear of the forest, which dates from the war. Flames, like
odors, bring back memories, says Bardamu, reducing the Prous-
tian concept of involuntary memory to a hazy recollection of
childhood which is just barely comforting, and which certainly does not transcend temporality. Bardamu has surrendered
to a childish impulse to destroy the hut which gave him pain-
ful memories, to protest against the company which had exploited him, against Robinson who had stolen all the money
and left him alone in the jungle, against the jungle which
surrounded him and held him prisoner. He does not seek to

regenerate the past in order to stand outside time; he destroys memory's dirty bandages, leaving a cleaner past in which little Bardamu and his uncle watch the telephone company burn down. He has recreated a childhood experience already purified by faulty memory. The action of the flames, like writing, wipes out the unpleasant present, reinstates an agreeable but inaccurate past.

Bardamu enjoys the odor of the fire because it brings back memories. But the purifying quality of fire, as Bachelard tells us,[2] is at least partially due to its ability to deodorize. Instead of deodorizing, Bardamu is creating a voluminous quantity of malodorous smoke. In the same way Céline kindles a flame (writes) which creates an unpleasant smell (novels about vomit, defecation, war and disease). The novels themselves are full of odors.

The bombardment in Normance creates odors. This time it is an odor of burning people mixed with gunpowder and tar--a scene from hell: "c'est ça les Déluges, des odeurs et puis encore d'autres . . . des trouvailles . . . oh, un relent de viande grillée!" (N, 144: "that's how it is with Floods, odors and more odors . . . real finds . . . oh, a whiff of roasted meat!"). The opening scene in Guignol's Band, also a bombardment, brings out the roasted meat image again with a baby "tout cuit à point" (G-B, 17: "done to a turn"). In Nord we meet the fleeing prostitutes who build a fire in a hole in the plain to roast the Rittmeister's horse, "que ça sent si fort!" (Nord, 609: "what a stench!"). Céline's fire departs from both of the purifying qualities noted by Bachelard (deodorizing and cooking) because his fire creates odors and the flesh that is cooked was not originally intended to be eaten. "La viande cuite représente avant tout la putréfaction vaincue."[3] ("Cooked meat represents above all putrefaction vanquished.") But the idea of "cooked people" interrupts the natural process of putrefaction without either facilitating digestion or achieving a civilized victory over food's swift decay. Fire harms people; they are not meant for burning. Céline's novels deliberately attack people, serve them up to themselves "done to a turn." The works are fiery, and they sear.

At the same time, the works have a purifying quality. By transforming garbage and distasteful subjects into art, Céline succeeds in exalting humankind's dirty linen, for he certainly does not destroy it. People produce an inordinate quantity of filth; this is an age-old subject of literature. This, then, is true alchemy: from such stuff to create literary flames of lasting value.

Céline's writing may have accomplished this very object on a personal level. To burn away the trash of memory, to protest against all the companies and encircling forests which have enslaved us and held us prisoner--who would not set fire to a houseful of soaked socks with that in mind? As we have seen, the flame is the word. Other writers (Anaïs Nin, Simone de Beauvoir) have professed more openly the cathartic value of writing. Céline offers the cleansing experience as an excuse for pyromania.

Après moi, le volcan

Céline's love for the ocean, boats, harbors, and rivers has been much noted: Danièle Racelle-Latin sees the boat as the dominant image in Voyage;[4] Gilbert Schilling considers water the dominant element.[5] "He who dreams water cannot dream fire," says Bachelard,[6] and it must be admitted that in Céline's water-ruled world fire behaves much like water. Even taking into consideration that certain metaphorical combinations of fire and water are literary conventions (such as torrents of light, a rain of fire, the sunset over the ocean), Céline's novels include an unusually large number of fire/water couplings and, in Normance, repeated references to the bombardment as a modern-day Deluge. The flames cascade, inundate, splash, surge. The sky melts, the Seine boils, molten cataracts pour down at Jules' command: "C'est une inondation de feu," "des vraies cataractes de lumière!" "les cascades du ciel!" "de vrais torrents," "un fleuve," "tout Paris en mer de feu!" (N, 59, 75, 41, 57, 39: "It's an inundation of fire," "true cataracts of light!" "the cascades of the sky!" "true torrents," "a river," "all of Paris a sea of fire!").

The doctor hypothesizes in Nord that Berlin is under heavy attack, and the underground Reichsgesundt has probably been destroyed. All of Berlin, the doctor supposes, has become a volcano. Within the volcano, Grünwald is a lake of fire. This lake of fire reminds us of the Finnish baths, which were part of the womb-like atmosphere. They have now been transformed into their antithesis, a crater.

> Berlin est tourné volcan . . . que c'est un grondement perpétuel . . . Grünwald doit être un lac de feu, les demoiselles au fond, et les télégrammes! . . . et le cratère des bains finlandais . . . (Nord, 455)

> (Berlin has turned into a volcano . . . there's a steady rumbling . . . Grünwald must be a lake of fire, the ladies at the bottom, and the telegrams! . . . and the crater of the Finnish baths . . .)

From a distance, the noise and fireworks of constant bombardment create an impression the doctor sums up as that of an imaginary volcano. Combining the water he remembers with the fire he believes to have replaced it, he comes up with the image "a lake of fire," clearly an apocalyptic image where incompatible elements merge. In Normance, however, the flood from the sky is not described from a distant point of view; it is directly overhead. It resembles nothing so much as a volcanic eruption, as Céline does not hesitate to say.

> . . . au moins quatre immeubles qui sautent! le bruit de bouchon: vlaouf! . . . et un cratère à leur place, tout de suite! . . . qui rejaillit! une lave, des torrents de lave qui fusent! haut! haut! éclaboussent autour tout le quartier! [...] et le métro! submergés! . . . il doit faire chaud sous le tunnel! . . . ils y sont tous! . . . toute la place bouillonne de «Bengale» . . . un volcan d'éclaboussures! (N, 55-56)

(. . . at least four buildings exploding! . .
. like the sound of a cork: pop! . . . and a
crater in the spot, right away! . . . spurt-
ing up! lava, torrents of lava flowing!
high! high! splashing all over the neighborhood! [...] and the metro! submerged! . .
. it must be hot in the tunnel! . . . they're
all there! . . . the whole square boiling
with "bengal fire" . . . a volcano of
splashings!)

The first hint of the importance of the volcano image is

the dedication of Normance: "à Pline l'Ancien" ("to Pliny

the Elder"). Frédéric Vitoux points out that the dedication

makes a flattering comparison between Céline and Pliny the

Elder, emphasizing the author's innocence as a dedicated

chronicler.[7] As the doctor explains,

Saquez pas le probe chroniqueur! . . . regar-
dez un peu Pline l'Ancien, il a fallu des an-
nées, qu'il se décide à son grand moment . .
. qu'il aille renifler la Vésuve! (N, 208)

(Don't give the upright chronicler the sack!
. . . take a look at Pliny the Elder, it took
him years to make up his mind to his moment
of glory . . . to go take a sniff at Vesuvius!)

As Vitoux points out, Pliny was the one who wanted to observe

the eruption of Vesuvius close at hand. But he is also the

one who went to Stabiae to save the inhabitants who were

threatened by the volcano. Pliny then died, asphyxiated by

the noxious fumes. The doctor seems to see himself as a lat-

ter-day martyr, a chronicler of disaster--specifically, of a

volcanic eruption--who has suffered from his devotion to sci-

entific observation. One of the problems, of course--and one that he recognizes fully when he insists that he is inventing nothing--is whether the chronicler only observed the eruption, as he claims, or whether, like Jules, he actually provoked it. The problem is a crucial one for Céline, repeatedly accused of collaborating. The doctor may place the responsibility for the cataclysm on a perfectly unadmirable character--Jules--still, it is not only clear that Jules is performing the work of the artist (as is the doctor), but it is also obvious that the doctor identifies with him.

> . . . c'est pas une petite histoire de faire raffluer les Déluges, de nous faire foncer dessus charges sur charges des quatre horizons! au doigt! . . . zessayez! zessayez un peu! Vous allez dire que je me régale, que je suis un cataclyste aussi! (N, 107)

> (. . . it's no small thing to recall the Floods, to bring charge after charge down on us from the four horizons! with a wave of his hand! try it! just try it! You'll tell me I'm wallowing in it, that I'm a cataclyst myself!)

The entire novel justifies the label. To mitigate his condemnation and enhance the role of "cataclyst," the doctor compares Jules to Noah, pointing out that the Flood was nothing next to this inundation of fire. Noah is a savior; we can only hope the artist is too.

Bardamu's burning of his jungle hut is in reply to a deluge, and he too is compared to Noah. The combination of the drenching rain and Bardamu's fever makes everything appear to be melting. Everything is losing its shape, its ri-

gidity, its solidity.   Everything is returning to the state
of primal chaos.

> Tout fondait en bouillie de camelotes, d'es-
> pérances et de comptes et dans la fièvre aus-
> si, moite elle aussi.   Cette pluie tellement
> dense qu'on en avait la bouche fermée quand
> elle vous agressait comme par un bâillon
> tiède.   Ce déluge n'empêchait pas les animaux
> de se rechercher, les rossignols se mirent à
> faire   autant   de   bruit   que   les   chacals.
> L'anarchie partout et dans l'arche, moi Noé,
> gâteux.   Le moment d'en finir me parut arri-
> vé. (V, 175)

> (Everything was melting into a puddle of
> junk, of hopes, and of accounts, and with the
> fever too, it too was damp.   This rain so
> dense your mouth felt forced shut when it
> came at you as if with a lukewarm gag.   The
> downpour didn't stop the animals from getting
> together, the nightingales started making as
> much noise as the jackals.   Anarchy all
> around and in the ark me, Noah, doddering.
> It seemed to me the time had come to put a
> stop to it.)

The feverish Bardamu finds it hard to distinguish between
things; the fire in his body shows everything about him in
its chaotic state, although the hut still forms an artificial
barrier between himself and the rain.   Taking the situation
into his own hands, the false Noah burns the ark, the parti-
tion between him and anarchy.   By burning the hut he burns
the rain's "lukewarm gag," and his fire is a form of speech.
His message is that nothing but illusion separates us from
chaos.   The night-rain is life, the fire a flicker illuminat-
ing the flood, which might otherwise not be seen.   The novel
is the fire, really a torch in the darkness.   Céline writes
with a purpose: to show us that the world does not conform

to the structure we conventionally give it, that we are in fact surrounded by anarchy. In any case this is the structure of his fictional space, the imaginary landscape through which his pícaro journeys and from which he gathers the material for his books. These books are the fire in the night.

Moths

> Pendant que nous parlions des nègres, les
> mouches et les insectes, si gros, en si grand
> nombre, vinrent s'abattre autour de la lan-
> terne, en rafales si denses qu'il fallut bien
> éteindre. (V, 168)

> (While we were talking about niggers, the
> flies and other insects, so big, in such num-
> bers, fell upon the lantern in clouds so
> thick that we had to put it out.)

One insect fluttering around a lamp at night is a nuisance, but a cloud of bugs, drawn by the light and falling dead in droves, is more than inconvenient; eventually the light must be put out. The racial slur implied in this passage is appropriate to the Africa sequence. The colonists consider the native population on a plane little higher than insects.

People too are drawn to fire, even when it means their own death. Bardamu admits that it was a suicidal attraction to fire that made him join the army: "j'étais pris dans cette fuite en masse, vers le meurtre en commun, vers le feu. . . " (V, 17: "I was caught up in this mass flight, toward shared murder, toward the fire. . . "). Inevitably, fire attracts large numbers of insects seemingly bent on self-destruction; war has the same effect on humans. People are often compared to insects in Voyage, but never more appropriately than in the description of their mindless rush to war. It is not the fire alone that attracts people; they are actually drawn to death--their own or someone else's. Friends

and relatives gather to watch a man die, and their swarms under the lights remind one of flies: "Et comme il y en avait
des parents!   Des gros et des fluets agglomérés en grappes
somnolentes sous les lumières des «suspensions»" (V, 297:
"And what a lot of relatives there were!   Fat ones and thin
ones stuck together in dozing clusters under the ceiling
lights"). The fascination of fire is at least partially the
fascination of death.

The fascination with the work of art is similarly linked
to death. The work itself is considered "alive" as long as
it holds the interest of our contemporaries; in fact, we are
likely to say it is "still" alive, as if the fact were sur-
prising. Some works, of course, are never alive at all, in
any sense; others have a lively appeal, but not because of
any resemblance to our experience of life. The fundamental
image of Voyage au bout de la nuit is that life is a journey
through night; the secondary image of art as a flame reinforces the idea that the work gives another perspective, illuminates the night in at least a limited way. This does indeed bestow a certain conventional kind of immortality on the
work: it is a torch that can be rekindled long after the
death of the author.   In this respect the fascination with
the work of art is also linked with death.

Céline's remarks on the cinema reveal a tendency to regard it as escapist, but he has much more respect for the illusions of the movie theater than for the commonly accepted
illusions of love. As Bardamu watches a film, he feels again

the fatal attraction of the moth to the lantern: "Alors les
rêves montent dans la nuit pour s'en aller s'embraser au mirage de la lumière qui bouge" (V, 201: "Then dreams rise into the night to go catch fire from the mirage of moving
light"). The film, like a novel, is the fire that sets the
dream ablaze. It is not like life. The well-lighted theater
is compared to a cake, the people pressing about it to larvae: "c'était comme tout le contraire de la nuit" (V, 345:
"it was like the exact opposite of the night"). The movie is
illusion, but it sheds some light on reality.

> Ce n'est pas tout à fait vivant ce qui se
> passe sur les écrans, il reste dedans une
> grande place trouble, pour les pauvres, pour
> les rêves et pour les morts. (V, 201)
>
> (It's not quite alive what's going on up on
> the screens, there's a large indistinct patch
> left, for the poor, for dreams and for the
> dead.)

The cinema is unquestionably a positive dream-producer.
"C'est ça qui est bon! Quel entrain ça vous donne! J'en
avais ensuite, je le sentais déjà, pour au moins deux jour-
nées de plein courage dans la viande" (V, 201: "That's really great! What a boost it gives you! I could already tell I
had a good two days of courage under my belt"). The spectator derives courage from the screen to face the dark outside.
It is the part of the film that is "not quite alive" that
makes these dreams possible.

For its creator as well, the work has the fascination of
death. Writing is like dying. The writer is spearing some-

thing within himself and fixing it at the end of his pen. Showing it to a reader has some of the morbid quality of exhibiting the corpse of a suicide to the public. Not only does the writer feel himself bleeding as he writes; he feels that every phrase, once set down, destroys the possibilities for growth in another direction; the possibilities become fewer and fewer until the whole work is pinned down, no longer palpitating, to become what each reader chooses to make of it. The reward for the whole grisly business is that the work has the power to light up the night.

After all, fire is not always fatal; it also warms, like the war in <u>Voyage</u>: "La guerre avait brûlait les uns, réchauffé les autres, comme le feu torture ou conforte, selon qu'on est placé dedans ou devant" (<u>V</u>, 216: "The war had burned some, warmed others, just as fire tortures or comforts, depending whether you're inside it or in front of it"). The author is inside, the reader happily toasting himself in front of the fire. It is significant that although the work burns, it is not consumed. One of the few things not damaged by the thorough bombing in <u>Normance</u> is the doctor's book. The apartment building is a shambles, fire is everywhere, but his papers do not burn: "et que ça avait pas brûlé! . . . le plus drôle!" (<u>N</u>, 341: "and it hadn't burned! . . . strangest of all!"). The concierge gathers together the papers which are blowing in the street: chapters from various books mixed in with old bills and letters. This is Céline's final comment on the book; it is a disconnected and intensely personal mixture of odd papers blowing down the street for anyone to catch hold of. We may discard them or use them to light a fire (literally or spiritually), as we choose.

Sorcerers (and Apprentices)

Almost by definition, the pícaro is an apprentice. Bardamu had prepared for the hut-burning by an apprenticeship in the art of fire-making, just as any artist practices his craft.

> Malgré que je fusse maladroit naturellement, après une semaine d'application je savais moi aussi tout comme un nègre, faire prendre mon petit feu entre deux pierres aigües. (V, 173-174)

> (Despite my natural awkwardness, after a week of applying myself I was able, just like a nigger, to start a little fire with two sharp stones.)

He lacked the time to become adept at striking the stones: "Beaucoup d'étincelles me sautaient encore dans les yeux" (V, 174: "Lots of sparks flew into my eyes"). With sparks in his eyes, Bardamu is building a fire, as if the coruscating eyes themselves made the fire catch. The fire-maker is in a position of great power; the writer who sees himself as a fire-maker is not belittling his role.

Jules has more than shining eyes; his entire body gleams. "Le moulin brille à présent, luit! [...] Jules aussi luit sur sa plate-forme! reluit!" (N, 42: "The mill is shining now, gleaming! [...] Jules too is gleaming on his platform! glistening!"). Jules looks as if he were on fire. He sends off sparks; he has caused the conflagration. "--Regardez-le donc! ses doigts! les bouts! vous voyez pas les étincelles?" (N, 109: "Just look at him! his fingers! the tips! don't you see the sparks?") Jules appears to be a sorcerer cursing the city. Jules "emperor of flames," Jules pointing a flaming finger at the clouds and calling down a rain of fire shows us an imposing picture of the artist-prophet.

The doctor-narrator also sees himself as a prophet, one of the denouncing variety. "Y a des dénonceurs de périls! je suis de ceux!" (N, 91: "There are denouncers of dangers! I'm one of 'em!") The doctor's excuse for his flamboyant, jerky style is that the nature of his material--catastrophe-- and his role as universal scapegoat require just such an emotional style.

> J'ai pas de cinéma personnel pour vous faire voir le tout assis . . . confortable . . . ou comme dans un rêve . . . ni de bruitage non plus . . . ni de critiques rémunérés aptes à me vous tartiner mille louanges du tonnerre de Dieu de mes génies! . . . j'ai que l'hostilité du monde et la catastrophe! . . . je perds la catastrophe je suis perdu! (N, 121)

> (I don't have a private movie theater so you can see it all while you're sitting . . . at your ease . . . or like a dream . . . no sound track either . . . no well-paid critics to slap on a thousand words of praise of my God's truth genius! . . . all I have is the world's hostility and catastrophe! . . . if I lose the catastrophe I'm finished!)

Without cinematic effects or paid-off critics to persuade the public to like him, the writer must rely on showmanship, and disaster makes a good show. In any case, his message of denunciation is perfectly sincere. He does not need Jules' power to summon disaster to be able to see catastrophe in Europe's future. He believes that his fire enables him to foresee what is to come, particularly the consequences of war.

The writer's clairvoyance makes him an excellent leader and pathfinder. Such is the position of the doctor in the last novels as he wanders through Germany in search of refuge. He organizes every aspect of the journey and protects his little band (wife, friend, cat) from the sometimes contained, sometimes savage hostility surrounding them. His expression of the loneliness and uncertainty of his position can be poignant:

> vous diriez de l'encre notre sous-bois . . .
> y a que là-haut les nuages qui sont illumi-
> nées, brillants . . . des pinceaux des cent
> projecteurs et des reflets d'autres explo-
> sions . . . Nord . . . Est . . . mais dans
> notre parc nous, rien . . . l'encre . . .
> deux pas . . . trois pas . . . vous vous sen-
> tez devenir tout ouate, tout nuit, vous-même
> . . . un moment vous êtes étonné de chercher
> encore, quoi? . . . vous ne savez plus . . .
> (<u>Nord</u>, 501)

> (our woods seem like ink . . . it's only the
> clouds way up that are lighted, bright . . .
> the beams of a hundred searchlights and re-
> flections from other explosions . . . North .
> . . East . . . but on our grounds, nothing .
> . . ink . . . two steps . . . three steps . .
> . you feel yourself going cottony, all dark-
> ness yourself . . . for a moment you're sur-
> prised you're still searching, for what? . .
> . you don't remember . . .)

The use of the second-person pronoun and the sense of dis-solving into the night universalize the experience described

and include the reader, even though the repeated "ink" implies that he is describing the loneliness of the writer. We
are all seekers. Céline is not so arrogant as to suggest
that he is the only one looking for something--a path, an an-
swer. He merely suggests that of all those seeking, he alone
knows which direction to go. In this he is descended from a
long line of poets and writers who sincerely believed that
the role of the artist is to point the way. Victor Hugo's
radiant poet is just one example:

> Il rayonne! il jette sa flamme
> Sur l'éternelle vérité!
> Il la fait resplendir pour l'âme
> D'une merveilleuse clarté.
> Il inonde de sa lumière
> Ville et désert, Louvre et chaumière,
> Et les plaines et les hauteurs;
> A tous d'en haut il la dévoile;
> Car la poésie est l'étoile
> Qui mène à Dieu rois et pasteurs![8]

> (He beams! He sheds his radiance on eternal
> truth! He makes it shine for the soul with a
> wondrous luminance. He floods with his light
> city and wilderness, palace and hovel, both
> plains and peaks; to all from above he un-
> veils it; for poetry is the star that leads
> to God kings and shepherds!)

Céline's purpose is not to lead the people to God, but to
force them to recognize the reality and finality of death.
His position as Cassandra ("denouncer of dangers") is not
likely to win him great popularity, but he is upheld by the
certainty that he is right. For Hugo, poet, message, and medium all cast light, illuminate the future, point the way.

For Céline too the writer is a pathfinder, flame-thrower, seer, wizard.

Pyrography

Borokrom's very name comes from his ability to make bombs. His propensity to throw them is another matter. The first incident takes place in a bar, where Joconde is responsible for a brawl. After escaping from the hospital, she seeks out Cascade in a bar and begins ripping the bandages from her buttock wound. She inflames the dockers gathered in the bar; under the impression she is being mistreated, they attack Cascade and begin to destroy the bar. Boro starts the barrel organ to add to the din, then throws a grenade. The explosion effectively breaks up the fight and they all escape.

Boro turns on the organ and throws the grenade at the same time because he uses them to the same effect: to create a diversion; and the key word here is create. Borokrom makes music and bombs; both inspire an intense emotional reaction in his companions. As a performing artist, his task, like the writer's, is to create an emotional response. Céline himself insisted that conveying emotion was the main purpose of his writing. Borokrom is an incendiary, as is Céline, in his way.

The second bomb also permits Boro to escape, and especially to destroy the evidence of Claben's murder. He shuts Delphine and Ferdinand in the basement with the dead body.

Just as Ferdinand forces the trap-door open, an object is thrown inside and explodes:

> Brrouum!! . . . Un tonnerre qu'éclate dans le noir! . . . là en pleine cave! . . . en même temps! . . . en plein bazar! . . . Ah! c'est féerique! . . . plein la gueule! . . . Je suis écroulé sous les décombres . . . C'est lui qu'a jeté le truc! Maudit chien . . . une explosion formidable! . . . Encore lui! (G-B, 215-216)

> (Boom! . . . A clap of thunder bursting in the darkness! . . . right in the cellar! . . . at the same time! . . . right in the mess! . . . Ah! it's marvelous! . . . Right in the kisser! . . . I'm crumpled under the rubble . . . He was the one who threw the thing! Dirty dog . . . a terrific explosion! . . . Him again!)

Once again we are struck by the parallel between Borokrom, the bomb-throwing piano player, and Jules, the bombardment-provoking painter. Borokrom obviously uses bombs to help him escape; it is less easy to understand the motivation of Jules making a holocaust of Montmartre. The doctor suggests that Jules is a frustrated ceramicist looking for a kiln:

> lui qui parlait toujours de son four! qui souffrait de pas avoir un four . . . un four «grand-feu»! je le trouvais servi! . . . qu'il nous montre un peu sa maîtrise s'il était si artiste au four! (N, 231)

> (he was always talking about his kiln! suffering from not having one . . . a "hot" kiln! He got what he was asking for! . . . let him show off his mastery if he's such an artist at the kiln!)

Jules is, in fact, displaying his artistry with a colossal flame-show; the light beams sweeping across the sky are, after all, "pinceaux" ("paintbrushes"). The doctor himself is exercising his artistry in describing the light show. Page after page is filled with colors; the lights are compared to jewels, flowers, delicate lace. At this point the creative arts of the painter and writer fuse: the bombardment is their masterpiece. The doctor tells us, "faudrait être artiste pour vous faire voir les couleurs . . . la palette . . . " (<u>N</u>, 53: "I'd have to be an artist to make you see the colors . . . the palette . . . "). Modestly, the narrator professes to be a simple "chronicler," unequal to the task of rendering the fireworks in the sky. Any of a number of brilliant quotations would give him the lie; the following is representative:

> une cataracte d'or d'en haut . . . un fleuve
> des nuages . . . jaune . . . et puis vert . .
> . c'est pas commun comme masse de feu ce qui
> cascade, rejaillit, inonde . . . je vous en
> ai raconté pourtant . . . mais là vraiment
> c'est le ciel entier qu'on dirait qui fond .
> . . et puis d'en bas on voit des rues qui
> s'élèvent . . . s'enlèvent . . . montent en
> serpents de flammes . . . tourbillonnent . .
> . tordent d'un nuage à l'autre . . . une
> église entière qui part, se renverse, tout
> son clocher pointu, brûlant, en espèce de
> pouce! . . . c'est extraordinaire! renversé
> sur nous! . . . l'Eglise d'Auteuil! . . . je
> vous l'ai raconté! . . . à l'envers . . .
> mais elle, pas si flambante tout de même . .
> . plutôt en reflets . . . ah vous voyez c'est
> pas semblable . . . vogue! s'envole! . . .
> c'est que je suis pas artiste peintre, je
> vous rends mal l'effet . . . (<u>N</u>, 56-57)

(a cataract of gold from above . . . a river
from the clouds . . . yellow . . . and then
green . . . it's a most unusual mass of fire
which cascades, spurts, floods . . . I've described a few to you . . . but this time
really it's the entire sky that seems to be
melting . . . and then from down below we see
streets lifting up . . . flying away . . .
mounting in serpents of flame . . . whirling
. . . twisting from one cloud to the next . .
. an entire church that takes off, overturns,
its pointed spire all on fire, like some sort
of thumb! . . . it's extraordinary! over-
turned above us! . . . the Eglise d'Auteuil .
. . I told you about it! . . . upside down .
. . but it wasn't so very fiery after all . .
. more like reflections . . . ah you see it's
not the same . . . it sails! flies off . . .
it's just that I'm not a painter, I don't
render the full effect . . .)

The writer writing about the painter painting produces an extraordinary work of art. Neither the narrator nor Jules
works in a customary medium, but together they are producing
a very modern masterpiece. Their collaboration is all the
more impressive because involuntary; the doctor never stops
denouncing Jules. At one point he compares Jules' real
painting unfavorably to his sky painting; as an ironic condemnation of surrealistic painting the intent--and the ef-
fect--is to form a highly laudatory word-picture couched in
derogatory language:

Je l'avais vu vernisser ses toiles . . . moi
parfait plouc, aucune autorité d'art, je
m'étais dit à moi-même: il le fait exprès!
il bluffe le bourgeois! il leur peint des
autobus sur la mer de Glace . . . et les
vaches paissant des couteaux! . . . des lames
d'acier! des poignards en fait d'herbe ten-
dre! . . . maintenant il nous sorcelait autre
chose! [...] c'était plus terrible que ses

gouaches!   c'était un petit peu plus osé!
(N, 62-63)

(I had been to his openings . . . hick that I
am, no art authority, I had said to myself:
he's doing it on purpose! he's pulling the
wool over their eyes! he paints them busses
on the Sea of Ice . . . and cows grazing on
knives! . . . steel blades! daggers in place
of tender grass! . . . now he was cooking us
up something different! [...] it was more in-
credible than his gouaches! quite a bit more
daring!)

The sky painting is indeed bolder, but not significantly different in style. The upside-down church, the sky melting into a golden cataract, the streets mounting in serpentine
flames to the clouds, are the living, moving, colorful off-
spring of the bus on the sea of ice and the cows grazing on
steel blades. The difference in medium is, however, significant. By substituting fire for paint, the artist attributes
god-like qualities to himself, especially when he uses fire
to paint the heavens, where only the sun or Zeus' thunder-
bolts should provide color. Since fire can be equated with
the word, the sky-painting is essentially a linguistic image,
and we have not merely a writer describing a painting, but a
writer describing the artistic scope of language. The visual
effects alone are spectacular. When the writer becomes incendiary, his novel will have an explosive effect.

Arson is not restricted to musicians, painters, and
stranded feverish anti-heroes. Two women in Nord, the paraplegic's wife and the bookkeeper's wife, are caught trying to
set fire to the manor after the mysterious cesspool murders.

In the middle of the night the doctor hears a noise on the stairs and surprises them as they are about to set the building on fire. He himself had suggested burning the place soon after he arrived. "Ce qu'arrangerait bien, qu'on les brûle tous!" (Nord, 487: "What would work out best would be to burn them all!"). The instinct to burn one's troubles away is almost as strong among Céline's characters as the impulse to push a troublesome person into the nearest hole. Simply walking down the street Sosthène becomes enraged at the drab clothes of the people around him and shouts, "Mais il faudra qu'on les brûle! . . . Qu'on les incinère!" (G-B, 276: "They must all be burned! . . . incinerated!"). All of these would-be arsonists are indulging in fantasies about a cleaner world, purified of whatever trash is annoying them at the moment. The rage they feel is translated into physical terms as fire. The same burning emotion rages throughout Céline's novels. He is as much an incendiary as Jules or Borokrom.

Jules' work of art is not just a display of fireworks for people to gape at on the fourteenth of July; it is an air attack, part of a war. The bombing is a form of expression. Jules, the id-figure, creates a very beautiful work of art expressing anger, aggression, and the urge to destroy. Certainly Céline does nothing less with his novel. Céline sees himself as a painter of destruction. Not only does he depict the destructive forces already existing (war, poverty, death), but he sees creation as stemming from destruction:

he is Jules calling the bombers, directing them, setting the fire.

Fire consumes; destruction is the subject and, in a sense, the work of the artist. Céline's novels directly attacked French literary conventions of vocabulary, syntax, and, of course, punctuation. He did not see the writer as the staid guardian of the purity of French letters, but rather as a bomb-thrower.

The space in which Céline's imaginative adventure takes place has been shown to be divided between labyrinth and underground; it is, for the most part, dark.[9] What light there is has a watery quality, like the diluted light at Rancy soaking into the ground: "La lumière du ciel à Rancy, c'est la même qu'à Detroit, du jus de fumée qui trempe la plaine depuis Levallois" (V, 238: "The light of the sky in Rancy is the same as in Detroit, smoke juice soaking into the plain from Levallois on"). Fire, however, has a special significance; it brightens, it destroys, it cheers and wounds. The written work does all of these things. The writer creates that fire; he is a god (Jules is like a malevolent caricature of Hephaestus, the lame god of fire), a sorcerer, and an incendiary. Céline's picaro, as represented by his successive narrators, is obsessed with movement and with lighting fires. His movement is exploration. It leads to a knowledge of his space he feels compelled to communicate. His final gesture, the summing up of his life and experience, is the novel which he casts like a bomb in the face of the public.

Notes

1Les Structures anthropologiques de l'imaginaire (Paris: Bordas, 1969), p. 198.

2Gaston Bachelard, La Psychanalyse du feu (Paris: Gallimard, 1938), p. 202: "Le feu purifie tout parce qu'il supprime les odeurs nauséabondes." ("Fire purifies everything because it does away with nauseating odors.")

3Bachelard, p. 202.

4"Symbole et métaphore idéologique dans Voyage au bout de la nuit," Australian Journal of French Studies, 13, No. 1-2 (1976), 88.

5"Images et imagination de la mort dans le Voyage au bout de la nuit," L'Information littéraire (1971), 74.

6Bachelard, p. 178: "L'eau et le feu restent ennemis jusque dans la rêverie et celui qui écoute le ruisseau ne peut guère comprendre celui qui entend chanter les flammes: ils ne parlent pas la même langue." ("Water and fire remain enemies even in the world of fantasy, and he who listens to the brook can scarcely understand one who hears the song of the flames: they don't speak the same language.")

7Bébert, le chat de Louis-Ferdinand Céline (Paris: Grasset, 1976), p. 51.

8Victor Hugo, "Fonction du poète," in Les Rayons et les ombres.

9Allen Thiher, in Céline: The Novel as Delirium (New Brunswick, NJ: Rutgers Univ. Press, 1972, p. 12), says, "Anyone lost in the darkness of the journey will have no light by which to see how things are. Moreover, the voyage through darkness means not only not seeing things; it also means being caught up in the madness of this world without light of any kind."

V

WAITING FOR DAWN

Most people sleep at night. The narrator of <u>Nord</u> is unable to sleep because of a constant buzzing in his ears, one
of the side-effects of a war wound. For years he has lived
with this internal noise which keeps him awake. Every night
he lies quietly in bed, dozes a little, and waits for day-
break: "je peux passer des heures, moi, allongé, sans dormir
. . . j'ai l'habitude, j'écoute mon tintamarre d'oreille . .
. je sais attendre le jour" (<u>Nord</u>, 430: "I can spend hours
stretched out without sleeping . . . I'm used to it, I listen
to the din in my ear . . . I know how to wait for day"). He
passes night after night in this fashion; he is awake for any
emergency, and he has time to think about possible solutions
to the problems facing him.

Bardamu experiences a similar state of insomnia when he
goes to work at the insane asylum at the end of <u>Voyage</u>. Memories of the events in Toulouse (the death of old lady Henrouille) keep him awake for hours. He jumps out of bed and

paces the room until morning. He predicts that he will never again sleep with an easy conscience.

There is some suggestion, in both these cases, that eternal wakefulness is the only way to deal with a hostile world. Bardamu says, "J'avais perdu comme l'habitude de cette confiance, celle qu'il faut bien avoir, réellement immense pour s'endormir complètement parmi les hommes" (V, 419: "I had lost the knack of that confidence, the kind you have to have, absolutely enormous, to sleep soundly among other men"). The loss of confidence in people, beginning with the loss of his "virginity to horror" in the war (V, 17), is a process continuing the length of the Voyage, and in the succeeding novels there is no longer any question of trusting anybody.

Sleep erases the consciousness of passing time; sleeplessness accentuates this consciousness. Donald O'Connell points out that Céline's works are devoid of dates or exact references to time,[1] and the absence of clocks and calendars leaves the actors in an indeterminate flow of time. There is also considerable hesitation--waiting introduced within waiting--marked by the points of suspension intended to convey the frequent pauses in everyday speech. While the novels' narrators display a lucid awareness of the present that the other characters do not share, any time other than the present seems not to exist.

This chapter will deal with the concept of time experienced as an inability to sleep: a wakeful waiting for dawn.

Hours of waiting inevitably lead to frustration. This frustration and attendant sense of impotence may eventually account for the hostility surrounding the narrator which requires him to lie awake--a sort of vicious circle in which waiting gives rise to more waiting.

Sleepless nights have an end--the dawn. To the prisoner awaiting execution the end is final. Since we are all condemned to die, waiting for the dawn is a universal experience. In the long run the person waiting may look forward to the end, even if he fears it, because he is tired of waiting.

People become restless from waiting; they move around aimlessly to keep busy. Traveling is one of the ways of dealing with the boredom of waiting. Céline also suggests that one may spend the time thinking, planning, and preparing for the problems one is certain to meet. His final alternative is to write: writing is a form of mental travel and fills time in much the same way.

Salle des pas perdus

Robinson chooses to wait until after the wedding to con-
summate his marriage with Madelon. It is his own idea. Madelon's romantic illusions do not include premarital fidel-
ity, and while waiting, she has an affair with Bardamu. "A
lui donc l'éternité et à moi le tout de suite" (V, 386: "So
eternity was for him and right now was for me"). Since for
Bardamu there is no eternity, the immediate pleasure is all-
important.

Bardamu once believed in waiting. When he was living
with Musyne he used to wait in the kitchen for her after the
private concerts she gave, which were sometimes quite pro-
longed. As he felt her slipping away from him he began to
spend more and more time waiting for her, perhaps believing
that such proof of devotion would be rewarded. He compared
himself to a dog that didn't want to lose its bone. He wanted to sleep, but instead he waited. Although Musyne was pa-
tently deceiving him (the servants took him for a pimp), Bardamu waited. Finally Musyne left him, and Bardamu learned
that his waiting was to go unrewarded. During an air alert
he preferred not to spend the night in the butcher's cellar
and offered to wait for her upstairs. He waited a night, a
day, a year--she never returned. After this experience Bardamu no longer waits for his pleasures; he will make a cuck-
old of his friend and say, "Right now was for me."

The author seems in fact to be irritated by the resigned acceptance with which people wait not only for their pleasures, but even for necessities. Poverty and social oppression are accepted as part of the human condition, and people spend their lives in miserable circumstances because they believe what they have been told: that love is supreme happiness (and will come in the future), that the greatest honor is to die for one's country (and be decorated posthumously), that the trials of life prepare us for the life to come (and we buy a place in heaven with our patience).

The failure of love is amply illustrated in <u>Voyage</u>, from Bardamu's several unfortunate affairs to Robinson's inability to come to an understanding with Madelon. Robinson lashes out against love just before he dies: how is it possible, he asks, that people simply believe what they are told, and despite all evidence, wait patiently for the wonderful things that are supposed to happen?

> Ça te suffit de répéter tout ce que bavent les autres [...] ça te suffit parce qu'ils t'ont raconté les autres qu'il y avait pas mieux que l'amour et que ça prendrait avec tout le monde et toujours . . . Eh bien moi je l'emmerde leur amour à tout le monde! (<u>V</u>, 483)

> (You're satisfied to just repeat the pap you hear from others [...] you're satisfied because the others have told you that there wasn't anything better than love and that it would work for everybody and every time . . . Well I say fuck their love for everybody!)

Robinson berates Madelon for believing in words; she clings

tenaciously to her love for him because she believes that

things will get better in the future. But the future is

merely a word, since it is beyond experience. Of course the

novel itself is nothing but words; the novelist, because he

deals in words, knows how suspect they are. Robinson's

awareness is better than that of the average person when he

points out that language must be analyzed, not simply swal-

lowed at face value.

Words account for patriotism too, and Bardamu has no pa-

tience with a mother who passively accepts her son's depar-

ture for war:

> Elle était heureuse de me retrouver ma mère,
> et pleurnichait comme une chienne à laquelle
> on a rendu enfin son petit. Elle croyait
> aussi sans doute m'aider beaucoup en m'em-
> brassant, mais elle demeurait cependant infé-
> rieure à la chienne parce qu'elle croyait aux
> mots qu'on lui disait pour m'enlever. (V,
> 94)

> (My mother was happy to see me again, and she
> whimpered like a bitch whose puppy has been
> given back to her at last. I'm sure she
> thought she was helping me out when she
> kissed me, but she remained inferior to the
> dog because she believed in the words they
> used to take me away from her.)

Again Bardamu compares a person waiting to a dog, symbol of

faithfulness and devoted patience. Bardamu has little re-

spect for dogs, but he has even less respect for his mother,

because the dog is not deluded by the explanations which per-

suade his mother that it is morally right to send her only

son to war. Under these circumstances, language is an insid-
ious instrument wielded by those in power. In the same way
that the people's belief in the future is turned to advantage, the ethical implications of nationalism are blurred and
distorted by linguistic manoeuvering.

Céline condemns all attempts to make the waiting appear
worthwhile, all efforts to sweeten the medicine. He has
nothing but contempt for priests, who see life as a waiting
room for heaven:

> D'après son idée à lui, on était tous les hu-
> mains dans une espèce de salle d'attente
> d'éternité sur la terre avec des numéros. Le
> sien de numéro excellent bien sûr et pour le
> Paradis. (V, 373)

> (According to his own idea, we were all of us
> humans on this earth in a sort of waiting
> room for eternity with numbers. His own num-
> ber was of course an excellent one and guar-
> anteed entry into Paradise.)

Céline sees life as a waiting room, but not for heaven.
There is nothing after the end.

Alcohol is another palliative Céline cannot condone. He
considers sex a harmless physical diversion by no means worth
waiting for, liquor a dangerous physical and mental irritant
to be avoided at all costs. Water is lacking in Normance, so
the tenants drink a great deal of alcohol, making it impossible for them to observe what is going on:

> tous ces locataires pleins de gniole verront
> jamais rien . . . j'attendrai que le robinet
> rejute! . . . C'est la volonté ou la mort,
> moi, mon genre! qu'on se le dise! comme

Pline! . . . je veux pas observer dans
l'ivresse! et nous sommes en plein Déluge .
. . et pas d'eau! (N, 215)

(all these tenants full of booze will never
see anything . . . I'll wait for the faucet
to spurt again! . . . Self-control or death,
that's my style! take note! like Pliny! . .
. I don't want to be drunk when I'm observ-
ing! and we're in the middle of a Flood . .
. and not one of water!)

The fiery deluge cannot be observed properly by those who
drink, distorting their perceptions. The doctor has already
indicated that he sees things others don't: "he's halluci-
nating, the cantankerous old fart!" (see p. 102). This is
one of the passages where the doctor makes it clear that his
vision is special; even Lili, who was on the roof with Bébert, does not seem to have seen the same things, and Norbert, who was in the next building, denies seeing anything of
the kind. This willful confusion of detail and the presentation of contradictory and misleading information are characteristic of Céline's portrayal of reality. His narrator's
view is privileged. Certain witnesses to the events are obviously unreliable because they were drunk at the time. Others were not even present; they were underground. Those who
drink "will never see anything"; fire-water blinds, and only
he who abstains can see.

Fire alone, however, is a necessity for which one cannot
wait. It is more important than eating. In the woods, for
example, "manger peut toujours attendre! . . . mais la pre-
mière nuit sans feu vous attrapez la mort" (Nord, 369: "eat-

ing can always wait! . . . but the first night without fire
you catch your death"). Fire is the one essential in the
night, the only thing people cannot do without. We have already "caught our deaths," but we can look forward to a more
comfortable night with fire. As we have seen, the role of
art can be that of a warming fire, and writing is one form of
self-deception Céline favors.

Although people wait more or less patiently under certain circumstances, at other times they become impatient, and
this impatience, too long contained, can make them intracta-
ble or openly malicious. Bardamu attributes the viciousness
of the people he meets in Africa to their endless wait for
cooler temperatures. "Tout le monde devenait, ça se comprend
bien, à force d'attendre que le thermomètre baisse, de plus
en plus vache" (V, 125: "While waiting for the thermometer
to drop, everybody was becoming more and more shitty, it was
perfectly understandable"). The most extreme example of
pent-up hostility coming to the surface in people who wait is
the behavior of the passengers on the Amiral Braqueton.
Cooped up with one another for weeks at sea, they become
bloodthirsty and look for a scapegoat. Bardamu does not expect to escape alive. "Le temps passait et il est périlleux
de faire attendre les corridas" (V, 117-118: "Time was passing and it's dangerous to make people wait for their bull-
fights"). The passengers refuse to wait any longer; their
frustration has reached an intolerable level.

The culmination of frustration which has no immediate outlet may be a self-induced sexual release. Masturbating has the advantage of relieving tension without disturbing anyone else. According to Bardamu however, it is not sufficient:

> j'avais beau me retourner et me retourner encore sur le petit plumard je ne pouvais accrocher le plus petit bout de sommeil. Même à se masturber dans ces cas-là on n'éprouve ni réconfort, ni distraction. (V, 199)
>
> (no matter how much I tossed and turned on the little mattress I couldn't capture even a wink of sleep. Even masturbating in such cases brings neither consolation nor diversion.)

He does fantasize a great deal, and perhaps the phonetic proximity of "oneirism" and "onanism" gives the two activities a psychological nearness of particular value to the writer. Bardamu dissipates the frustrated energy he has been holding in by day-dreaming and, as a story-teller, by writing. Céline rejects all forms of mental delusion which make life easier to live, including religion, patriotism, love, and liquor, but he likes to write.

Firing Squad

One of Ferdinand's friends was taken from the military
hospital and shot at dawn. Dawn is normally a time of ambiguous significance: it is the end of the night and the beginning of the day. For the man who is executed, it is unequiv-
ocally the end; there is no new day. The night Robinson and
Bardamu meet, they remain together to watch the sun rise:
"Une longue raie grise et verte soulignait déjà au loin la
crête du coteau, à la limite de la ville, dans la nuit; le
Jour! Un de plus! Un de moins!" (V, 49: "A long gray and
green stripe was already underscoring the crest of the hill
in the distance, at the edge of town, in the night; Day! One
more! One less!"). Dawn marks the boundary of the night.
It is the mnemonic notch reminding one that a day has been
completed and another waits to be lived. While it appears to
be a beginning, from the perspective of the present it can
only be an end, since, as Bardamu well knows, there is no future.

The psychological future is usually closely linked to
the psychological present and the psychological past. All
three of these mental scenarios are repeatedly contradicted
by everyday experience. Optical illusions, memory gaps, and
misreported or misconstrued information are just a few of the
obstacles to accurate representations of the present and
past. Only the present is supported by verifiable sensory

perception. The future is a purely mental construct which corresponds so rarely to experience that correct predictions of the most trivial events are occasion for remark. If waiting is the mode of the present, and the future is projected as a continuation of waiting, that which ends waiting blots out the future. When Robinson asks Bardamu if he intends to return the following night, Bardamu replies, "Il n'y a pas de nuit prochaine" (V, 49: "There is no tomorrow night"). It is futile to make plans for a next night which will take shape only when it is no longer to come.

In Normance the dawn is both the end of the night and the end of the bombardment. "C'était l'aube, c'était la fin" (N, 245: "It was the dawn, it was the end"). There will certainly never be another night like the one just past, since it is unique to the doctor's imagination. In this sense its end has the finality of death, and Normance (whose name gives the title to the novel) will soon be tossed down the elevator shaft to prove that the imaginative venture ends in death.

There are various ways of meeting death; some are entirely unacceptable. Bardamu finds it monstrous that his colonel should await death as calmly as if he were meeting a friend.

> Il se promenait au beau milieu de la chaussée et puis de long en large parmi les trajectoires aussi simplement que s'il avait attendu un ami sur le quai de la gare, un peu impatient seulement. (V, 16)

(He was walking around smack in the middle of
the road, up and down among the bullet-paths
as free and easy as if he were waiting for a
friend at the railway station, just a touch
impatient.)

Bardamu does not consider death a friend. In any case he is
aware that his friends are very likely to be the ones who
kill him: "des millions d'hommes, braves, bien armés, bien
instruits, m'attendaient pour me faire mon affaire et des
Français aussi qui m'attendaient pour en finir avec ma peau"
(V, 81: "millions of men, brave, well-armed, well-educated,
were waiting for me to do me in, and Frenchmen too were waiting to bump me off"). Bardamu is not merely waiting to die;
he is waiting to be shot by his countrymen. The same fear
subsists in the doctor's mind when he avoids taking shelter
in the metro because the crowds will lynch him. "Waiting for
dawn" is more than a sleepless night, more than an awareness
that death lies inevitably at the end of life; it is the specific haunting image of the condemned man waiting for the
firing squad.

Early in Voyage Bardamu recognizes that he is playing a
waiting game. He has seen active service during World War I;
his girl friends have exhorted him to be brave and die for
his country; his mother has already given him up for lost.
He sees that there is no alternative--it is merely a question
of time.

A deux reprises ainsi on m'avait déjà recon-
duit vers les endroits où se parquent les

otages.   Question de temps et d'attente
seulement. Les jeux étaient faits. (V, 97)

(Twice now I had been escorted to the places
where hostages are parked. It was a simple
question of time and of waiting. The die was
cast.)

The battle front is where the hostages are "parked," also, by association, the place where the "Parques" do their work, cutting the thread of human life. From the time of the classical respect for the fates, through the Middle Ages with its ideal of courtly love and the implacability of Fortune's wheel, a common literary stance has been the acceptance and even glorification of the frustration involved in waiting. Submitting to the will of the gods or admiring his lady from afar, the hero of these literary worlds knows that the human condition requires patience and resignation to be borne. The literature of rebellion, on the other hand, teaches us that people have only to reject their fetters in order to assume their rightful sovereign position in life. Thus in our recent literature we have Camus, who believes in human brotherhood (with reservations), Sartre, who tells us that an individual must commit himself to a cause and take responsibility for his acts, and Proust, who assures us that a person's ability to retain, in memory, his former selves, and to recapture them with a sip of tea, delivers him deliciously from the tyranny of time.

Céline's fiction does not belong to the tradition which praises self-restraint, nor does it join the group singing the dignity of the individual. It belongs to the category in which people are of small account ("bags of larvae"), but he insists that people should protest rather than submit to fate. Basically, _any_ praise of people is false, but this should not be used as an excuse for weakness and self-delusion.

When the waiting begins to seem long, even for a disagreeable end, one response is to desire that end, to long for death: "on en avait comme envie de ce doux pays de mort" (V, 357: "you were almost longing for this gentle land of death"). The reference is to a popular song in which the phrase "au doux pays du rêve" ("in the gentle land of dream") appears. In this melancholy frame of mind the familiar image of the grave as a bed is remarkably appealing to the figurative insomniac: "on se penchait alors . . . pour se coucher dans le vrai lit à soi, vrai de vrai, celui du bon trou pour en finir" (V, 357: "you bent over then . . . to lie down in your own true bed, the really true one, the good old hole in the ground to have done with it"). Even in a mood where he is reconciled to dying, Bardamu must reproach people for living a quiet shadowy life of waiting:

> On la reprenait en choeur, tous, la com-
> plainte du reproche, contre ceux qui sont en-
> core par là, à traîner vivants, qui attendent
> au long des quais, de tous les quais du monde
> qu'elle en finisse de passer la vie, tout en
> faisant des trucs, en vendant des choses et
> des oranges aux autres fantômes et des tuyaux
> et des monnaies fausses, de la police, des
> vicieux, des chagrins, à raconter des ma-

chins, dans cette brume de patience qui n'en
finira jamais . . . (V, 357)

(We all took up the refrain again, the plain-
tive reproach, against those who are still
around, dragging their days, waiting along
the quais, all the quais in the world, for
life to get itself over with, doing things at
the same time, peddling to the other ghosts
oranges and stuff, influence and counterfeit
money, police, perverts, problems, spinning
tales, in this never ending mist of patience
. . .)

The fact that the living are referred to as ghosts shows a

lack of distinction between the quick and the dead, and the

futile activities of those ghosts are so shrouded in fog they

cease to hold any meaning; people sit idly on the banks as

life flows by. Unconscious of death, they are unconscious of

life. They are also unaware that, long before dying, they

harbor the maggots that will feed on their corpses. Since

they are incapable of imagining their own deaths, they do not

know that they can be defined as worm-houses. This is one of

Céline's most important messages; the dawn, and with it

death, arrives for everyone, but only those who are aware of

it are really living.

Mais le colonial il est déjà tout rempli
d'asticots un jour après son débarquement.
Elles n'attendaient qu'eux ces infiniment la-
borieuses vermicelles et ne les lâcheraient
plus que bien au-delà de la vie. Sacs à lar-
ves. (V, 116)

(But the colonist is already filled up with
maggots a day after getting off the boat. He
was all they needed, and these hard-working
little worms won't let go of him until well
beyond death. Bags of larvae.)

The ghosts sitting on metaphorical quais quietly selling oranges to other ghosts await an end which for them has already come, since they can scarcely be considered to be alive.

Terminus

What does one do while waiting? What is the best use of time, since there is a single inevitable end for everyone? The long hours may be used to travel, to think, or to write, and in fact, these three activities seem to be equated. Waiting makes people restless; they may go for a walk in order to occupy themselves and give themselves the impression of doing something with their time. The ceaseless movement in these novels is partly a fear reaction to the pressure of constant surveillance (real or imaginary), partly an attempt to give significance to otherwise empty time. While waiting for Musyne, Bardamu walks about the neighborhood where they live. Immobile, one feels lost, purposeless, helpless. Any sort of movement gives some sense of direction. The movement may be aimless and futile, but it places one, labels him as "a person who is going somewhere." As Bardamu puts it, it is impossible to be nowhere: "Il fallait bien être quelque part en attendant le matin, quelque part dans la nuit" (V, 27: "After all you had to be somewhere while waiting for morning, somewhere in the night").

Bardamu has determined to explore the night in order to discover just exactly what there is about it that frightens the people around him. Everyone he approaches pushes him away, so that the wandering he had undertaken to be on the move and avoid trouble turns into a deliberate search for the reason behind this rejection. At any rate, anything is better than staying in one place and waiting patiently for the end.

> «Courage, Ferdinand, que je me répétais à moi-même, pour me soutenir, à force d'être foutu à la porte de partout, tu finiras sûrement par le trouver le truc qui leur fait si peur à eux tous, à tous ces salauds-là autant qu'ils sont et qui doit être au bout de la nuit.» (<u>V</u>, 219)

> ("Courage, Ferdinand," I said to myself over and over, to bolster myself up, "after being kicked out of every place you're sure to find out what it is that scares them so much, assholes that they are, and which must be found at the end of the night.")

Bardamu is continually rejected--after all, the pícaro is by definition an outsider. He uses this rejection as an excuse to keep moving, and the motivation it gives him justifies his travels.

Not only his body, but also his mind, needs to be in motion. While he walks about he thinks and dreams, reflects on his situation, philosophizes about the things he sees. Bardamu considers mental activity essential. When he decides to leave Molly, she points out that he will no longer be able to stroll about and let his thoughts wander night after night, as he loves to do. The doctor too likes to occupy his mind while his wife sleeps in <u>Nord</u>: "je passe pas des nuits, tant de nuits, à réfléchir, pour ne pas à peu près tout prévoir" (<u>Nord</u>, 555: "I don't spend the nights, so many nights, in thought, without foreseeing just about everything"). The doctor is constrained by circumstances to lie still, but his mind is constantly active; thinking is an appropriate activity for the time spent waiting.

After traveling and thinking to fill time, one may turn to writing. Céline's narrators have all traveled and reflected on their travels before deciding to write down their story. By retelling an adventure they have supposedly lived through (and they insist that their tale is true: "J'invente rien," <u>N</u>, 32: "I'm not making anything up") they inaugurate a double journey--the tangled reconstruction of a past experience, and the act of narrating that memory. This journey does not involve genuine physical movement, but it imitates that movement; the world in which it moves is an artificial construct retaining some of the features of the original, so that the reader experiences the psychological, rather than the literal truth of the narrative. For example, the narrator of <u>Normance</u> uses a device he has copied from life--he makes the reader wait.

> C'est terrible ce que j'ai oublié! . . . je
> vous ai pas raconté le «centième . . . » le
> «millième» du bombardement! mais vous perdez
> rien pour attendre! je vais vous retrouver
> un peu plus tard! (<u>N</u>, 192)

> (It's terrible how much I've forgotten! . . .
> I haven't told you a "hundredth . . ." not a
> "thousandth" of the bombardment! but you're
> not missing out on anything by waiting! I'll
> catch you up on it a little later!)

Céline's narratives are regularly interrupted by delaying incidents: hallucinations, derogations of his publishers, imaginary conversations with his reader, who tires of the lengthy digressions. The imaginary interlocutor is always aggressively displeased, so that the narrator is required to justify himself. The doctor gives the impression that he is harried, even in the manuscript, by the hounds of the labyrinth. After transferring the waiting experience to the reader, the doctor resumes his narration ("Why we never made it to the metro"), interpolating a waiting incident of an entirely different nature.

By breaking down the wall and crawling into the next building, the doctor discovers his friend Norbert sitting at a table sumptuously set. Norbert's gaze is fixed, he does not hear his friends call his name, and he appears to be waiting for something. A few minutes later he seems to awaken, and seeing them before him he smiles and says, "Je vous attendais!" (N, 324: "I've been waiting for you!"). Under the circumstances he could not possibly have been expecting them, so it seems reasonable to assume that he is using a pat phrase to hide his embarrassment at being temporarily disoriented. But it soon becomes obvious that he is not just disoriented; he is completely detached from his surroundings. When his friends speak of the recent bombardment he says they are crazy and denies that anything has happened, but intimates that important events are about to take place: "il ne s'est rien passé, voyons! . . . chutt! chutt! . . . il va se passer! [...] ils vont venir! je les attends!" (N, 325: "oh come on, nothing has happened! . . . shh! shh! . . . it's going to happen! [...] they're going to come! I'm waiting for them!"). After the doctor, Lili, and Ottavio explore the apartment, finding a dead woman in the bathtub and another in the kitchen, the doctor insists that Norbert explain who is expected to come. Norbert whispers some momentous names which the doctor repeats incredulously: "et pas que le Pape qu'il attend! Churchille et Roosewelt! qui vont venir! là! qu'il me dit" (N, 347: "and not just the Pope he's waiting for! Churchill and Roosevelt! they're coming! here! that's what he says").

It is curious that Norbert's dissociation from the reality of the narrator is so complete that his physical surroundings remain unharmed by a bombardment that has destroyed everything in the vicinity. It occurs to the reader to wonder if Norbert is really crazy, or if he may not be right in saying, "Nothing has happened," since the doctor has already given ample reason to question his own testimony. Norbert's behavior makes him appear to occupy an alienated corner of a crazy world, fragmented in such a way that the apocalypse the doctor has described as present and past is placed by Norbert in the future. Even with the temporal sequence rearranged, this world is consistent with its own laws, one of which is that time is experienced as waiting, another that no matter how pointless movement seems to be, the framework of the novel automatically patterns the movement as journey, the journey as quest.[2] In Normance, the doctor's itinerary (little more than several trips up and down the stairs) takes on epic significance as he recounts it.

Writing, as a form of mental voyage, is an acceptable way to spend one's time. It is a combination of thinking and traveling. Voyage introduces the metaphor of life as a journey ("Notre vie est un voyage," epigraph: "Our life is a journey") and is, at the same time, the first work in a series that is a journey, closing, although not completed, with Rigodon. Céline's novels, both individually and collectively, follow the pattern of a journey. Henri Godard sees Céline's major metaphor to be the novel as a journey made by the author and reader together, with the author as guide.[3] In some of the novels, such as Normance, physical movement is relatively restricted, but an abortive journey--the trip to the metro--is nevertheless undertaken. In fact, Céline's journeys are never completed: Ferdinand never leaves London for Tibet, the doctor never reaches the metro, he travels through Germany without finding asylum, Bardamu watches Robinson die but continues to live. The fact that the end is never reached shows the journey to be essentially endless, just as waiting, although it cannot exist without positing an end, must psychologically be perceived in the present with the end at some future time not yet reached. The traveling through space, either physical or mental, which constitutes the writing experience for the novelist is the subject of Céline's work. This space is the scene of a variety of adventures, many of them based on the moral ambiguity inherent in a social structure which rewards departures from its moral principles in the rich but not in the poor. The picaresque adventure we have followed has for its protagonist a novelist. His journey must, for the purposes of publication, be interrupted at some point. Each novel is a fragment of the journey; each tale is arrested before any end is reached; and at the death of the author the opus, still in movement, is cut short. There is a point after which there are no new beginnings, but that point cannot properly be called an end; it is a suspension . . .

Despite the travel theme of Céline's novels, their world is one of waiting: "y a que ça de vrai avec le monde, attendre!" (Nord, 489: "that's all that's true in the world, waiting!"). Waiting leads to feelings of boredom, frustration, impatience, and a transformation of fear--waiting for an undesirable end--into a longing for that end. The journey undertaken merely to be doing something becomes a mental journey when it is retold in a novel. In the space of the novel, waiting takes on a timeless quality, because it never ends. There is no sinister dawn, only "le baroque, le fantastique, la dérision hilare d'un interminable récit picaresque"[4] ("the baroque, the fantastic, the hilarious derision of an interminable picaresque narrative").

Céline did not vanquish time, but with a wave of his novelist-magician's hand he abolished it. His narrative remains unterminated and interminable, his imaginative journey halted, but unfinished.

Notes

[1] Donald O'Connell, _Louis-Ferdinand Céline_ (Boston: Twayne, 1976), p. 45.

[2] The same sort of Everyman quest may be seen in the novels of Claude Simon, Michel Butor, and Samuel Beckett. All of these quests derive from Leopold Bloom's heroic day in Dublin.

[3] "Les Références au travail narratif dans le roman célinien," _Australian Journal of French Studies_, 13 (1976), p. 16.

[4] Pol Vandromme, _Louis-Ferdinand Céline_ (Paris: Ed. Universitaires, 1963), p. 6.

CONCLUSION

Any reading of a novel is a journey through the imaginative space created by the novelist, a journey which is a
purely mental construct. The best of such constructs may be
of singular beauty and near-perfect symmetry, but they cannot
be expected to have much solidity. When I attempted to trace
an outline of my reading of Céline through certain configura-
tions of imagery, I discovered that much of the beauty, symmetry and fragility resided in the tension maintained between
opposites in every dimension: conscious space is a labyrinth, the synthesis of closed and open space, where there is
always somewhere to go, and choices are to be made concerning
direction, but one is always surrounded by walls. The most
important form of movement is falling, which is a synthesis
of mobility and immobility, for no effort of movement is required, yet one arrives at another place. Subconscious space
is the underground, a synthesis of external and internal
space, since it is an internalization of the cavern, estab-

lishing a cave within a cave, where inside and outside are identical. The work of art is a fire in the night, the synthesis of light and dark. Finally, time is perceived as waiting, and waiting as the synthesis of temporality and non-temporality: there is a perpetual sense of time passing and of being removed from time.

When I attempt to transpose my reading, which is essentially a spatial construct, onto a series of numbered pages to be read in succession, I find that the structure does not easily adapt itself to sequential examination. Therefore I have arranged the five chapters in such a way as to reflect a journey which takes place entirely in the imagination and which echoes in certain ways the picaresque journeys of the protagonists.

I begin with the perception of conscious space as a labyrinth from which escape appears to be impossible. This is an imaginative perception based on such empirical clues as the maze of winding and branching corridors, tunnels, rivers and streets. The protagonist, no hero, feels himself constantly pursued, persecuted, and spied upon. He encounters Minotaurs at every turn--death, the self, the city, and the fearful monster which the labyrinth can be. Wily woman, who once guided Theseus out of the labyrinth with a thread as tenuous as life itself, has become a beautiful dancer who gives dangerous advice.

The narrator descends beneath the surface to subconscious space. The descent is abrupt, like a fall, and the

above and below are likened to the waking and dream worlds.
It is in describing the dream world that the protagonist becomes a narrator. He may attempt to destroy himself as part
of the plunge into nightmare, or he may push another character down the stairs or under a train, killing him. Even
within the fiction he has the same power of control over his
own existence as a writer has when he creates a literary
world.

The subterranean world is the underground of mythological repute. It appears attractive, but its womb-like atmosphere hides sharp and rending teeth. It has an infernal air
because it is there that people reveal their unsavory side.
It is above all an intestinal image, a vehicle for waste disposal, and the last stage in the digestive process, so similar to the creative process, in which the writer digests experience and produces the written work. The underground is
fertile, and its fruit is the novel.

The novelist's journey takes place in the metaphorical
darkness of nihilism, but the written word is a kind of fire
lighting up the night. The fire consumes garbage, performing
a cleansing action. It flows like lava, and Céline's version
of the apocalypse is a deluge of fire. Fire draws insects to
their own destruction. All these images are treated as functions of the work of art. The role of the artist, or fire-
maker, is shown to be that of an incendiary, or of a prophet
who writes with letters of fire in the sky.

Time, in the Célinian imagination, is endless waiting. The sense of waiting is intensified in the many sleepless nights spent waiting for dawn. Dawn, as the moment of execution, is the moment of death. Death is the end of the journey which everyone awaits. Traveling is a way of dealing with the boredom of waiting; writing is a form of mental travel used to fill time.

The picaresque protagonist thus begins his journey in the labyrinth, descends to the underground, where he seizes his vocation as a novelist, flings his tale, a bomb of fire, at his reader, at the same time spinning out its narration as he waits for dawn, the annihilation of being. This is the final twist Céline has given to the picaresque form, which in his hands has become a distorted version of a version of the quest. From knights seeking the Holy Grail, through little boys stealing grapes from blind men, we have come to the artist hurling his brimstone-filled prophecies at the public. This Prometheus, who finds his fire in the underground and bestows it not as a beneficent gift, but rather as a terrifying warning, is not one of the heroes of old. In its journey, the quest itself has been transformed.

I cannot feel confident that in these pages I have set down in tangible form the shifting shape which is my reading of Céline. Convinced as I am that the structure can only be presented in truncated form, I consider this study a preliminary sketch. After taking such pains in my last chapter to show that there are no ends, I shall not pretend to end, but simply to stop.

BIBLIOGRAPHY

Only those works which were cited in the text, or which contributed significantly to it, are listed below.

Alméras, Philippe. "Du sexe au texte avec arrêt raciste." _Revue des Lettres Modernes_, No. 398-402 (1974), 81-103.

----------. "Nature et évolution de l'argot célinien." _Le Français Moderne_, 40 (1972), 325-334.

Bachelard, Gaston. _La Poétique de l'espace_. Paris: Presses Universitaires de France, 1957.

----------. _La Psychanalyse du feu_. Paris: Gallimard, 1938.

----------. _La Terre et les rêveries du repos_. Paris: José Corti, 1948.

Bataillon, Marcel. _Le Roman picaresque_. Paris: La Renaissance du Livre, 1931.

Beaujour, Michel. "La Quête du délire." _Cahiers de l'Herne_ 5. Ed. Dominique de Roux, Michel Beaujour, Michel Thélia. Paris: Pierre Belfond, 1968.

Bellosta, Marie-Christine. "_Féerie pour une autre fois I_ et _II_: Un Spectacle et son prologue." _Revue des Lettres Modernes_, No. 543-546 (1978), 31-62.

Blackburn, Alexander. _The Myth of the Pícaro. Continuity and Transformation of the Picaresque Novel 1554-1954_. Chapel Hill: Univ. of North Carolina Press, 1979.

Boissieu, Jean-Louis de. "Quelques effets 'littéraires' ou archaïsants dans Voyage au bout de la nuit." Revue des Lettres Modernes, No. 462-467 (1976), 33-51.

Brée, Germaine, and Marguerite Guiton. An Age of Fiction. The French Novel from Gide to Camus. New Brunswick, NJ: Rutgers Univ. Press, 1957.

Butor, Michel. L'Emploi du temps. Paris: Minuit, 1957.

Campbell, Joseph. The Hero With a Thousand Faces. 2nd ed., 1949; rpt. Princeton: Princeton Univ. Press, 1973.

Céline, Louis-Ferdinand. Casse-pipe. Paris: Gallimard, 1952, rev. for Collection Folio, 1970.

----------. D'un Château l'autre. Paris: Gallimard, 1957.

----------. Entretiens avec le professeur Y. Paris: Gallimard, 1955.

----------. Féerie pour une autre fois. Paris: Gallimard, 1952.

----------. Guignol's Band. Paris: Gallimard, 1952.

----------. Journey to the End of the Night. Trans. Ralph Manheim. New York: New Directions, 1983.

----------. Normance. Paris: Gallimard, 1954.

----------. Le Pont de Londres. Paris: Gallimard, 1964.

----------. Romans 1: Voyage au bout de la nuit suivi de Mort à crédit. Paris: Gallimard, "Bibliothèque de la Pléiade," 1962.

----------. Romans 2: D'un Château l'autre. Nord. Rigodon. Paris: Gallimard, "Bibliothèque de la Pléiade," 1974.

Chesneau, Albert. "Esquisse d'une conception de l'Histoire chez Céline." Australian Journal of French Studies, 13 (Jan.-Aug. 1976), 126-133.

----------. Essai de psychocritique de Louis-Ferdinand Céline. Paris: Archives des Lettres Modernes, 1971.

----------. "La Phrase de Céline dans ses rapports avec 'l'écriture organique.'" Problèmes de l'analyse textuelle. Actes du Colloque de Toronto, 1970. Paris: Didier, 1971.

Day, Philip Stephen. "Imagination et parodie dans <u>Voyage</u> <u>au</u> <u>bout</u> <u>de</u> <u>la</u> <u>nuit</u>." <u>Australian</u> <u>Journal</u> <u>of</u> <u>French</u> <u>Studies</u>, 13 (Jan.-Aug. 1976), 55-63.

----------. <u>Le</u> <u>Miroir</u> allégorique <u>de</u> <u>Louis-Ferdinand</u> <u>Céline</u>. Paris: Klincksieck, 1974.

Debrie-Panel, Nicole. <u>Louis-Ferdinand</u> <u>Céline</u>. Lyon: Emmanuel Vitte, 1961.

Durand, Gilbert. <u>Structures</u> <u>anthropologiques</u> <u>de</u> <u>l'imaginaire</u>. Paris: Bordas, 1969.

Eliade, Mircea. <u>Myths</u>, <u>Dreams</u> <u>and</u> <u>Mysteries</u>. Trans. Philip Mairet. New York: Harper and Brothers, 1960.

Fitch, Brian T. "Bardamu dans sa nuit à lui." <u>Bulletin</u> <u>des</u> <u>jeunes</u> <u>romantistes</u>, 8 (déc. 1963), 31-36.

Fletcher, Angus. <u>The</u> <u>Prophetic</u> <u>Moment</u>. Chicago: Univ. of Chicago Press, 1971.

Fortier, Paul A. "La Vision prophétique: Un procédé stylistique célinien." <u>Revue</u> <u>des</u> <u>Lettres</u> <u>Modernes</u>, No. 398-402 (1974), 41-55.

Frye, Northrop. <u>The</u> <u>Secular</u> <u>Scripture</u>: <u>A</u> <u>Study</u> <u>of</u> <u>the</u> <u>Structure</u> <u>of</u> <u>Romance</u>. Cambridge: Harvard Univ. Press, 1976.

Godard, Henri. "Un Art poétique." <u>Revue</u> <u>des</u> <u>Lettres</u> <u>Modernes</u>, No. 398-402 (1974), 7-40.

----------. "Les Références au travail narratif dans le roman célinien." <u>Australian</u> <u>Journal</u> <u>of</u> <u>French</u> <u>Studies</u>, 13 (Jan.-Aug. 1976), 7-17.

Guénot, Jean. <u>Louis-Ferdinand</u> <u>Céline</u> <u>damné</u> <u>par</u> <u>l'écriture</u>. Paris: Diffusion M. P., 1973.

Hanrez, Marc. <u>Céline</u>. Paris: Gallimard, 1961.

----------. "Céline, prophète au long cours." <u>Les</u> <u>Lettres</u> <u>Nouvelles</u> (sept.-oct. 1969), 165-172.

Hindus, Milton. <u>The</u> <u>Crippled</u> <u>Giant</u>: <u>A</u> <u>Bizarre</u> <u>Adventure</u> <u>in</u> <u>Contemporary</u> <u>Letters</u>. New York: Boar's Head Books, 1950.

Holtus, Günter. "Code parlé et code écrit: Essai de classification de la langue de Céline." <u>Australian</u> <u>Journal</u> <u>of</u> <u>French</u> <u>Studies</u>, 13 (Jan.-Aug. 1976), 36-46.

Homer. The Odyssey of Homer. Trans. Richmond Lattimore. New York: Harper and Row, 1965.

Hugo, Victor. Les Rayons et les Ombres, in Oeuvres poétiques I. Paris: Gallimard, "Bibliothèque de la Pléiade," 1964.

Huidobro, Vicente. Altazor. Santiago de Chile: Cruz del Sur, 1949.

Knapp, Bettina. Céline: Man of Hate. University, AL: Univ. of Alabama Press, 1974.

Krance, Charles. "Céline and the Literature of Extasis. The Virtuosity of 'Non-genre.'" Language and Style, 6 (1973), 176-184.

----------. "Semmelweis ou l'accouchement de la biographie célinienne." Revue des Lettres Modernes, No. 462-467 (1976), 7-32.

Kristeva, Julia. Powers of Horror. An Essay on Abjection. Trans. Leon S. Roudiez. New York: Columbia Univ. Press, 1982.

Lalande, Bernard. Voyage au bout de la nuit: Céline. Paris: Hatier, 1976.

La Quérière, Yves de. Céline et les mots; étude stylistique des effets de mots dans le Voyage au bout de la nuit de Louis-Ferdinand Céline. Lexington: Univ. Press of Kentucky, 1973.

Lewis, R. W. B. The Picaresque Saint: Céline as Novelist. Philadelphia: Lippincott, 1959.

McCarthy, Patrick. Céline. London: Allen Lane, 1975.

Matthews, J. H. The Inner Dream: Céline as Novelist. Syracuse: Syracuse Univ. Press, 1978.

Meyerhoff, Hans. Time in Literature. Berkeley: Univ. of California Press, 1955.

Nettelbeck, Colin W. "Un Art conscient: Structures, symboles et significations dans les derniers romans." Revue des Lettres Modernes, No. 462-467 (1976), 99-119.

----------. "Coordonnées musicales de l'esthéthique romanesque de Céline." Australian Journal of French Studies, 13 (Jan.-Aug. 1976), 80-87.

----------. "Temps et espaces dans _Féerie pour une autre fois._" _Revue des Lettres Modernes_, No. 543-546 (1978), 63-81.

O'Connell, Donald. _Louis-Ferdinand Céline._ Boston: Twayne, 1976.

Ostrovsky, Erika. _Céline and His Vision._ New York: New York Univ. Press, 1967.

----------. _Voyeur voyant: A Portrait of Louis-Ferdinand Céline._ New York: Random House, 1971.

Parker, Alexander A. _Literature and the Delinquent: The Picaresque Novel in Spain and Europe, 1599-1753._ Edinburgh: Edinburgh Univ. Press, 1967.

Plutarch. _Plutarch's Lives._ The Dryden Plutarch rev. by Arthur Hugh Clough. New York: E. P. Dutton, 1910.

Poulet, Robert. _Entretiens familiers avec Louis-Ferdinand Céline._ Paris: Plon, 1958.

Racelle-Latin, Danièle. "Symbole et métaphore idéologique dans _Voyage au bout de la nuit._" _Australian Journal of French Studies_, 13 (Jan.-Aug. 1976), 88-96.

----------. "_Voyage au bout de la nuit_ ou l'inauguration d'une poétique argotique." _Revue des Lettres Modernes_, No. 462-467 (1976), 53-77.

Richard, Jean-Pierre. _Nausée de Céline._ Montpellier: Fata Morgana, 1973.

Roux, Dominique de. _La Mort de Louis-Ferdinand Céline._ Paris: Christian Bourgois, 1967.

Sartre, Jean-Paul. _La Nausée._ Paris: Gallimard, 1938.

Schilling, Gilbert. "Espace et angoisse dans _Voyage au bout de la nuit._" _Revue des Lettres Modernes_, No. 398-402 (1974), 57-80.

----------. "Images et imagination de la mort dans le _Voyage au bout de la nuit._" _L'Information littéraire_ (1971), 68-75.

Smith, André. _La Nuit de Louis-Ferdinand Céline._ Paris: Grasset, 1973.

Spencer, Sharon. _Space, Time and Structure in the Modern Novel._ Chicago: Swallow Press, 1971.

Thiher, O. Allen. <u>Céline</u>: <u>The</u> <u>Novel</u> <u>as</u> <u>Delirium</u>. New
    Brunswick, NJ: Rutgers Univ. Press, 1973.

----------. "Le 'je' célinien: Ouverture, extase et clô-
    ture." <u>Australian</u> <u>Journal</u> <u>of</u> <u>French</u> <u>Studies</u>, 13 (Jan.-
    Aug. 1976), 47-54.

Thomas, Merlin. <u>Louis-Ferdinand</u> <u>Céline</u>. New York: New Di-
    rections, 1980.

Vandromme, Pol. <u>Louis-Ferdinand</u> <u>Céline</u>. Paris: Editions
    Universitaires, 1962.

Vitoux, Frédéric. <u>Bébert</u>, <u>le</u> <u>chat</u> <u>de</u> <u>Louis-Ferdinand</u> <u>Céline</u>.
    Paris: Grasset, 1976.

----------. <u>Louis-Ferdinand</u> <u>Céline</u>. <u>Misère</u> <u>et</u> <u>parole</u>. Pa-
    ris: Gallimard, 1973.

Whitbourn, Christine J. "Moral Ambiguity in the Spanish Pi-
    caresque Tradition." <u>Knaves</u> <u>and</u> <u>Swindlers</u>. Ed. Chris-
    tine J. Whitbourn. London: Hull Univ., 1974.

White, John J. <u>Mythology</u> <u>in</u> <u>the</u> <u>Modern</u> <u>Novel</u>: <u>A</u> <u>Study</u> <u>of</u>
    <u>Prefigurative</u> <u>Techniques</u>. Princeton: Princeton Univ.
    Press, 1971.

Widmer, Kingsley. "The Way Down to Wisdom of Céline." <u>Min-</u>
    <u>nesota</u> <u>Review</u>, 8 (1968), 85-91.

INDEX

This index includes authors and works cited, as well as thematic material not covered by the headings in the Table of Contents.